Saving the
Family Cottage

Saving the Family Cottage

A Guide *to* Succession Planning *for your* Cottage, Cabin, Camp *or* Vacation Home

Stuart J. Hollander, Esq.

Foreword by
Deborah Wyatt Fellows

PLEASANT CITY PRESS, LLC
Suttons Bay, Michigan
www.cottagelaw.com

For information, please contact Pleasant City Press, LLC
Post Office Box 490, Suttons Bay, Michigan 49682.

Printed and bound in the United States. First printing 2007.

ISBN 978-0-9793596-2-0

Library of Congress control number 2007924658

Cover and book design by Saxon Design Inc.
Author photograph by Rick Cover

To the families of Rex Terrace on Elk Lake,
where I learned the meaning of cottage

Contents

FOREWORD

I publish magazines about one of the beautiful places in the world. It's the kind of place that people who live elsewhere dream constantly about returning to and only feel their arrival is real when the landscape is populated with more trees than houses and the air seems somehow injected with pure and heady oxygen.

Of the many universal truths I've learned about places such as this, one of the most stunning is the collective pool of emotion and goodwill attached to the family cottage. It really is true that the silky threads of daydreams and laughter, serenity and joy weave their magic whether the cottage is nestled in the mountains or alongside a lake. People who have never experienced life at a family cottage sometimes accuse me of looking on that experience through rose-colored glasses. To which I reply that there is no need for glasses. The very light itself is magic.

I have spent a lifetime trying to distill the shared pieces of life at a cottage into some set of words and photos that would capture the experience on paper once and for all. Is it the welcoming embrace of an old lavender daybed where a book lies waiting in the yellow light of the screened porch? Is it days filled with woods and water and swimming rafts that bob and dip as each child's body is hurled toward the water with sheer abandon, frozen for just a moment in midair? Is it the meals of fresh corn and cucumber salads eaten outside, in laps or on weathered tables, as the evening sun, still high in the sky, filters through the trees as if through emerald lace? Is it the calm, the peace, the quiet when all of life's intrusions that seem so unavoidable at home are effortlessly held at bay? Is it the laughter? Surely it is the laughter that shrieks from the card table and bubbles up from the lake and drifts gently and softly out into the night like music from a distant piano.

When my siblings and I each chose to return to the region in which we had spent a part of every summer, I could find no explanation for this migration other than that we'd returned to the place where we had been happiest. As is true for so many families, the cottage was the elixir that brought our family closer together.

And so it is some kind of tragic irony that, when the time comes to discuss changes in ownership — say, when grandparents die and the cottage passes to the next generation — sorting out the particulars can shred the same family ties that the cottage made strong.

When cottage decisions rip families apart, the causes generally lie in a potent mix of emotion and dollars. Some members want to hang onto the cottage and keep rich traditions alive. Others want to sell the cottage and split the money — perhaps their lives don't allow them to use the place, and they want to cash out. If those wanting to keep the cottage cannot afford to buy it from the others, the family can be headed down a painful road of argument, resentment and even lawsuits.

Saving the Family Cottage is the tool families need to avoid all this. This book is a comprehensive guide that explains how, through careful planning, the gift of the cottage experience remains available for generations to come. Those families know that as the world moves faster and faster, as global economies and technology pull us further and further apart, there will always be a need for a simple place, bathed in sunlight and solace, that quite effortlessly brings us closer together.

Deborah Wyatt Fellows
Founder, *Traverse, Northern Michigan's Magazine*

INTRODUCTION

I live and practice law in Leelanau County, a beautiful corner of Michigan known for its turquoise waters, sand dunes, birch trees, and unspoiled Great Lakes beaches. I spend a lot of time advising people on cottage matters for a simple reason: more than a third of houses here are summer places.

As an estate-planning attorney (in my pre-enlightenment phase), I viewed the family cottage as a valuable asset that should be handled properly to reduce estate taxes and avoid probate. My clients normally directed me to distribute their assets (including the cottage) equally among their children, and offered no special instructions about the property's future. They rarely considered the risk that a child might leave or lose his inherited share of the cottage to a spouse (the dreaded "in-law"); the hardship imposed on a child who couldn't afford to pay cottage expenses; or the possibility of partition, the forced sale of the cottage by one owner. Instead, my clients seemed to possess an unspoken belief that everything would be fine between the children and future generations: "We know they will work it out — our kids may scrap but deep down they love each other."

The truth, however, is that descendants do not always work it out. I handled my first cottage partition lawsuit — a court-ordered sale of a cottage — in 1993. My clients, two cousins, were unhappy that a third cousin was squatting in a beach cottage they had all inherited. My clients had their own cottages nearby, did not need an additional cottage, and just wanted to sell. The squatter cousin, a social worker, could not afford to buy them out.

She decided to spend as much time in the cottage as she could before it left the family.

My clients wanted to know what they could do. Could they force the squatter cousin to sell the cottage? Yes, I told them. Because the cousins held title as "tenants in common," any co-owner could force the sale of the cottage.

I duly sent a demand letter to the squatter, who ignored it, so I filed a lawsuit seeking the sale. The squatter's lawyer confirmed that she had no defense to the lawsuit, and she finally agreed to list the property with a real estate agent. The property sold fairly quickly, and the cousins split the proceeds. They haven't spoken to one another since the cottage's sale in 1993.

In subsequent years, I continued planning estates for one set of clients (distributing cottages equally to children as tenants in common) while handling the occasional cottage partition case for others. One fall day, on my annual retreat to the Lake Superior shore, I was walking through the woods and a holy smoke thought popped into my head: *Why was I creating cottage tenancies in common if a forced sale — partition — was a possible outcome for the family?* (The cynics among you are probably thinking: "He's a pretty clever lawyer. First he charges them for the estate plan and then he charges their kids for the partition suit." Trust me: it ain't so.)

Following this troubling revelation, I decided to try to solve the cottage co-ownership and succession problem for my clients. First, I read everything written on the subject. I found only one relevant book: *Passing It On: The Inheritance and Use of Summer Houses.* Written in 1999 by the late professor Judith Huggins Balfe, this pioneering book describes sociological aspects of summer home ownership: patriarchal and matriarchal considerations, "cultural transmission," sibling rivalries, fairness, methods of dispute resolution, and inheritance norms. It is the first book to tackle why it is difficult to share and pass on summer homes. The book introduced to the cottage literature the terms "founders," "heirs," and "endowment." Professor Balfe, with her brother, Kenneth Huggins, an English professor, co-authored a companion workbook intended to help families with succession planning. Although the workbook provided useful questionnaires, it did not explain the deficiencies of tenancy in common, the perils of partition, or consider the suitability of the limited liability company for cottage ownership. These things, I felt, deserved more attention.

The absence of cottage-succession literature really surprised me, especially given the sheer number of cottages in North America (a number that is growing rapidly as baby boomers acquire second homes). There are 5.2 million vacation homes in the United States and about 600,000 in Canada. One of every twenty housing units in the United States is a cottage. One of every eleven Canadians has a cottage. These figures are likely to rise in the future as the baby boomers retire.

Well, I thought, given these numbers, maybe the small but steady number of partition suits I had seen in my law practice were not that big of a deal. Maybe there wasn't widespread cottage angst. Then I located a 2002 market research study that found that more than eighty percent of Canadian cottage owners planned to give their cottages to other family members. Of these owners, eleven percent said the cottage already had caused a rift within their families and, twenty-two percent believed the cottage would be a source of disagreement after the gift was completed. That meant a full third of Canadian cottage owners had experienced or expected family schisms due to the cottage. All this, before the cottage even changed hands. A recent law review article estimates that 130,000 potential partition disputes arise in the United States each year.

I haven't found Canadians to be particularly contentious, so if the Canadians were having cottage sharing and succession problems it was reasonable to assume a large number of Americans also faced the problem. So here we are: millions of people about to inherit an interest in the family cottage, yet they are not being told that taking title as *tenants in common* means *trouble is coming.*

If you inherited an interest in your cottage, it is very likely that you, your siblings, and your cousins share title to the cottage as tenants in common. If you are a parent thinking of passing your cottage down to your children and you don't take special steps, your children also will take title as tenants in common — something that is not in everyone's best interest.

This book will help you examine the succession options for your family and cottage. Here, I will outline the hazards of partition and tenancy in common — which places the rights of the individual owner above the family — and I will suggest a new way of thinking about your family cottage: as its own legal entity.

After studying this issue exhaustively, I recommend you transfer your cottage to a limited liability company, a relatively new organizational form. This business model will look at your cottage as a single entity with multiple members. The LLC is suited ideally to cottage sharing and succession planning because it allows us to switch the "individual owner comes first" bias inherent in common law forms of ownership to a "family comes first" bias.

I'll show you how to use the limited liability company to achieve your family's goals for the cottage, outlining techniques for management and power-sharing, scheduling, financing, graceful exits, and successful transfers that minimize federal taxes.

I am hopeful the following pages will help you share and pass your cottage on to future generations.

Terminology

Although I use the term "cottage" in this book, the succession planning principles for these properties are the same for Adirondack camps, hunting cabins, mountain lodges, hobby ranches, and other vacation homes. These terms are used throughout the book:

Branches are groups consisting of siblings and their descendants. See Chapter 9.

Cottage means a property that the founders wish to keep in the family indefinitely.

Cottage law describes the practice of law dedicated to cottage sharing and cottage succession planning.

Cottage LLC refers to a limited liability company established in connection with a cottage succession plan.

Cottage succession plan describes a legal framework designed to keep a cottage in the family over multiple generations.

Founders are the current owners of the cottage. Founders are not necessarily of the same generation, nor are they necessarily the people who originally purchased the cottage. If children or grandchildren of the purchasers own the cottage they are founders. The ownership interest of the founders places them at the center of the planning process: their ownership gives them the *right*, and, I might add the *duty*, to plan the future of their cottage.

Heirs are the intended *future* owners of the cottage. The term is not used in its legal sense.

I use other special terms in this book. The first time a term appears it is in **bold**. Terms are collected and defined in the glossary at the end of the book.

Key points are indicated with this symbol: ⚷

Author's Note

In this book I present several case studies. One is an actual partition case. Although my client granted permission to use information from her file in this book, I have altered names and details to protect other family members' identities. Other cases are composites drawn from years of legal practice. Still others are created by me to illustrate a point.

Legal advice is the application of law to specific circumstances. Please engage a qualified attorney before taking any action based upon what is written in this book.

The book recommends using a limited liability company for cottage succession planning. Every state and the District of Columbia has adopted limited liability company statutes, and so the type of cottage succession plan I recommend is feasible for cottages throughout the country. You should, however, confirm with your attorney that a limited liability company best meets your specific objectives.

With the exception of Louisiana, which derives its laws from the French Civil Code, the real estate law principles described in this book generally apply to cottages throughout the United States. States, however, can and do deviate from classic common law principles, so while the principles stated here generally are accurate, they may not describe the outcome under the law of the state in which your cottage is located.

As an American lawyer, I am not qualified to discuss Canadian law. The solution I propose for American cottage owners (the limited liability company) is not available to Canadians who own Canadian cottages. That said, the discussion of real estate law should be useful to the Canadian reader, because both the American and Canadian legal systems are based upon English common law. Some of the ideas in this book — scheduling methods, control allocation, dealing with the need of an owner to be bought out, and sanctioning a non-paying owner — will be useful to Canadian cottage families and their solicitors, and may be incorporated into a plan valid under Canadian law.

Cottages at Risk

Chapter 1

Trouble in Paradise

At Monica's family cottage, memories linger like ghosts: grandmother and her formality, fishing poles on the porch, sunlight on the lake, "Lassie Comes Home" moments, scavenger hunts and Monopoly till midnight. Today, Monica can walk into the cottage's toy closet and it still has that certain smell. "There are so few places in life that seem to not change so much," she says. "That is one of the reasons I love our cottage. It always stays the same."

And indeed, with proper estate planning, family cottages can be used by generation after generation, passed from hand to hand like a precious heirloom, to be filled with new memories, new little feet and new togetherness, as those revered elders smile down from the mantle.

Monica and her siblings came to me to create an estate plan that would keep her lakeside cottage in her family, so her children and their children's children can share sunny, lazy summer days together.

To achieve that, Monica definitely does need a plan — but not just any plan. She needs a new form of cottage succession planning that helps protect future generations from showdowns over everything from scheduling to selling the property. Too many cottages go from happy idylls to combat zones, with forced sales, severed relationships and siblings hurling letters like this at one another: "I am finished with this whole thing. I am tired of dealing with attorneys and you three. I want out now!" Hardly the stuff of sunlit memories.

The terrific appreciation of lakefront and view property in the past generation has changed the way some in the family view their cottage, making strife all the more likely. A cottage may be the most valuable asset a family owns. While some heirs think of cottages as sacred family retreats, others may resent having their inheritance tied up in the old place. Stepchildren and spouses who did not grow up at the lake often have weak emotional ties to the cottage but strong ties to its cash value. Some siblings never got along.

 All of this sets the stage for trouble in paradise. *Having no plan for the family cottage, or even relying on a traditional estate plan, makes the cottage and families vulnerable to turmoil.* My cottage plans change the way families own their interests in the cottage. Instead of holding a direct interest in cottage real estate, family members own membership units in a limited liability company (LLC), a relatively new form of business entity I describe in Chapter 8. The LLC owns the cottage real estate, the cottage furnishings, and perhaps the boats. Instead of transferring interests in real estate to their children, founders transfer the membership interests in the LLC to the cottage heirs. This method means the relationship of the members' children to the cottage is governed by the LLC operating agreement, not ancient common law doctrines.

The operating agreement determines everything about the cottage, including scheduling, contributions to expenses, permissible owners, renting, maintenance, and whether the property can be mortgaged. It prevents forced sales, but allows for graceful exits. Chapters 9 through 14 show you how to adapt the LLC operating agreement to your family's needs.

Time for a Plan

There is no time like the present to make plans for your cottage's future survival. Don't be tripped up by the most common reasons owners die without a plan. I've seen them all and none of them help when you are gone and your children (and the cottage) run into trouble. Common reasons to avoid making a cottage succession plan include:

THE REASON: Inability to solve an identified family problem. "John always argues with his brother but they both love *Lands End*. I don't know what I'm going to do."

THE REALITY: The cottage will probably deepen any discord between children and it may end up being sold.

THE REASON: Idealism. Parents want to believe that everyone will live happily ever after in the cottage. This relieves them of the need to plan. It will all work out just fine.

THE REALITY: The partition cases I've handled are proof that it doesn't always work out just fine.

THE REASON: Unwillingness to impose wishes on heirs. "I don't want to rule from the grave."

THE REALITY: Even children who can work together need a plan to avoid wrangling over scheduling, taxes, and maintenance. A founder who develops a plan in consultation with the heirs has the authority to make final decisions on how the cottage will operate. Often the founder will serve as a tiebreaker in unresolved debates between heirs.

The Reason: Lack of foresight. "What, me plan?"

The reality: Bad things are more likely to happen without a plan.

The Reason: Unwillingness to make the required effort or to incur the expense of developing a plan. "I'm giving them the cottage, isn't that enough?"

The reality: Founder-developed plans generally cost less than heir-developed plans because the founders (usually a married couple) are more likely to see eye-to-eye than their children. If you are giving them the cottage, finish the job and give them a plan to ensure they enjoy the cottage too.

The Reason: And the ultimate dismissal — a big shrug. "Hey, I'll be dead. It's not my problem."

The reality: True enough. How do you want to be remembered?

Many of my most successful clients are careful planners. Sometimes, however, planning is delayed or prevented by the perfectionist's instinct to address every eventuality. *Is your family better off with a perfect plan that is never implemented because it wasn't completed by your death, or with a pretty-darned-good plan that was completed in time to be binding?*

I often remind my clients not to let the perfect get in the way of the perfectly adequate. In other words, your cottage plan doesn't have to be perfect. Almost all of the planning methods described in this book may be revised during your lifetime. Most founders wisely allow their heirs to amend the plan after the founder's death to meet the family's changed circumstances or wishes.

FOUNDERS: please prepare a plan *now*. Your descendants will thank you for it.

The First Step

My mother had a pine sideboard that she just loved. She kept her precious china and glassware in it and dusted her treasures all the time. Mom really wanted me to have the sideboard and had already picked out the wall in my house where it would go. The only problem was I had never liked the sideboard. My house is Arts and Crafts, the sideboard Early American. Porcelain and glass don't excite me — perhaps a holdover from my days in earthquake-prone San Francisco. Sure enough, when Mom died I got the sideboard. I gave it away.

Imagine if, instead of a sideboard, it had been a share of a cottage. There are many good reasons why somebody wouldn't want a share of a cottage: the expense of maintaining it, bad memories, geography, a spouse's feelings, and (especially) a preference for the cash value it represents.

The cardinal rule of cottage succession planning is that, before giving it to a child, parents must confirm a child really wants a share of the cottage.

This is not as obvious or simple as it sounds. Parents love the cottage — if they didn't, they either would have sold it or made arrangements to sell it at their deaths. A parent's emotional ties to the cottage can blind the parent to the child's feelings about it. A parent may have a hard time understanding why his child might not want an interest in the cottage, even if it requires the child to make financial sacrifices (as the parent may have done to acquire and keep it).

Recently, a mother of three asked me to prepare a cottage succession plan. She was the third-generation owner and some of her grandchildren (who would be fifth-generation owners) already had fallen in love with the cottage. She wanted to be sure that the cottage would be available for them to use and ultimately acquire.

My client — let's call her Mary — must have had some hint that trouble was in the wind. She brought one of her daughters to our first meeting. The daughter expressed great love for the cottage and said she and her brother would want a share of it, but worried that her older sister, who had no children and lived far away, might not want any part of the cottage.

The childless daughter, Ann, attended our next meeting. She politely but emphatically stated she didn't want a share of the cottage. This seemed to take her mother by surprise. I reviewed Mary's financial statement and assured Ann that her mother would have the resources to give her cash rather than a share of the cottage. Ann, who entered the meeting quite anxious, left with a smile on her face. Mary left the meeting stunned, but later amended her estate plan so that Ann would not receive a share of the cottage. By forcing her children to reveal their feelings about the cottage, Mary surely averted great heartache within the family.

Chapter 2

Avoid the Worst:
A Partition Parable

In 1955, Paul and Rachel Meade bought 150 feet of frontage on Long Lake and hired a contractor to build a 1,400-square-foot cottage there, notable because its sole bathroom is accessible from each of four bedrooms and none of the doors lock. The family laughed about the gymnastics required to maintain one's dignity. The Meades and their children spent summer days at the white clapboard bungalow by the lake, where the screen door creaked and slammed, the kids raced off the dock, and everything was always sandy.

It was the family's own little seventh heaven. So, when the widowed Rachel died in 1989, she left the cottage equally to her four children in the standard way, as tenants in common.

And that's where things began to go wrong.

In fact, the Meade family's tribulations are a study in what can go very, very wrong with this traditional form of real estate ownership. Any tenant in common may force the sale of the cottage at any time. This is called the right to partition. It will be of great interest to those of you who currently own a cottage in this form or whose estate plans will result in your children owning your cottage as tenants in common (most of you).

The right to partition, which is the forced division of real property at the election of any of its owners, was recognized under English common law as early as 1540. This remedy was exported to the United States along with the rest of common law while we were a colony. The principle underpinning partition is that no person can be required to own property. Partition allows any co-owner of property to terminate his relationship with the other co-owners. The court will order this division if the property can be divided physically in a fair way. For instance, if two brothers owned a 160-acre farm, either one could seek partition. If the judge found that the farm could be split into two parts of equal value, the judge would order the division. Each brother would receive a deed to his 80-acre portion and they would not have to deal with each other again.

Assume, however, that the co-owned property was a small but highly valuable parcel of land, had one house on it, and four owners (*think cottage*). Because property such as this cannot be divided physically into four equal shares, the common law concluded that the only fair remedy would be to order the sale of the property, because sale would permit the court to divide the *proceeds* into four equal shares.

Natalie Meade fell in love with her husband, Frank Chen, in college and today he's a financially successful physician. She teaches high school English. The couple weren't able to have children and decided not to adopt. Despite Natalie's enthusiastic best efforts, she couldn't make Frank feel the same bond with her family cottage that she felt. Frank, who liked his lake time more than he did the idea of sharing a cottage with Natalie's siblings, persuaded Natalie to buy their own cottage on the same lake.

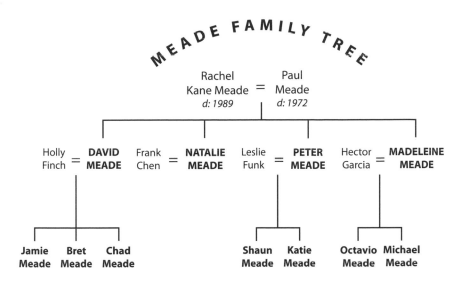

MEADE FAMILY TREE

Rachel Kane Meade = Paul Meade
d: 1989   d: 1972

Holly Finch = **DAVID MEADE**   Frank Chen = **NATALIE MEADE**   Leslie Funk = **PETER MEADE**   Hector Garcia = **MADELEINE MEADE**

Jamie Meade   Bret Meade   Chad Meade   Shaun Meade   Katie Meade   Octavio Meade   Michael Meade

The founders are indicated with all capital letters: MEADE
The heirs are indicated with boldface type: Meade
Deceased persons and in-laws are indicated with standard type

Frank did not pressure Natalie to sell her interest in the Meade cottage but made it plain he wouldn't mind if she did. Natalie countered that as an investment the cottage far out-performed his stock portfolio. Yes, he replied, but she was conveniently ignoring the annual payments they made for her quarter share of the cottage expenses.

Eventually Natalie came around to Frank's point of view. It didn't make sense to continue to pour money into a family cottage she never used. As hard as it would be to part with her interest, Natalie decided the time had come to ask her siblings to buy her out.

She was nervous about approaching her three siblings. An unspoken deal seemed to be in the air: she had become the wealthy aunt who, because she could afford her quarter share of the expenses, would subsidize the cottage during her lifetime so that it could be passed on to the next generation. Natalie wondered how her siblings would treat her if she asked to be bought out. Would they try to make her feel so guilty that she never would bring it up again?

That is exactly what happened. Natalie's less wealthy siblings pulled out all the emotional stops, pleading with her to retain her cottage share for the sake of the family, reminding her of its place in their childhood, asking, "What would Mom and Dad think?" Natalie didn't bring up the subject of a buyout for the next seven years, until her financial planner asked her.

"Why are you pouring money into a place you never use? Frank is going to retire in four years and it's time to start cutting back on unnecessary expenses. Your share of the cottage must be worth $200,000. We could put this money to better use."

So Natalie approached her siblings again, asking if they'd buy her share of the cottage.

When two university professors studied partition using the game theory developed by mathematician John Nash (subject of the movie *A Beautiful Mind*), they confirmed the common-sense notion that the amount one party should pay to "buy off" the other party (e.g. to prevent a partition suit) increases in proportion to how long the suit is likely to take and how much it will cost. In addition to math, the professors also discovered the unsavory side of partition, uncovering in one instance "a tale rife with family feuds, a shotgun wedding, contempt of court, nonpayment of legal bills, murder threats, secret transfers, piggeries, [and] snarling German shepherds …" In other words, just a typical partition case. For the rest of this story, please refer to the notes at the end of the book.

Her brother David, a lawyer with three boys, knew one thing: whatever happened, he would hang onto his share of the cottage. He was apprehensive about the cost, however, because his other siblings, Peter and Madeleine, who both adored the cottage, lived hand-to-mouth, and he found himself advancing their shares of the cottage expenses in lean years. David's sons each planned to go to college, but he hadn't socked away enough for the huge expense. He had hoped Natalie would not ask to be bought out, at least until he won his big case.

But Natalie was frustrated after years of keeping quiet about wanting to be bought out, and she was prepared to do whatever was necessary to resolve the problem, even if doing so meant risking the sibling relationships she so valued. At Natalie's request, a local real estate agent estimated the property's value at between $810,000 and $850,000. After subtracting the $20,000 mortgage, Natalie had reason to believe her quarter interest in the property was worth about $200,000.

Natalie offered to sell this interest to her siblings for $180,000. She felt this was generous. David, the only sibling who was willing to discuss the purchase with her, offered Natalie $100,000, which she rejected as too low. David did not respond to Natalie's offer to reduce her price to $160,000.

Madeleine, a married mother of two who lived in another state, didn't want to pay anything to Natalie for Natalie's interest. Madeleine believed that since Natalie didn't pay for the interest, had her own cottage (and no children to leave that cottage to), and was more financially secure than her siblings, Natalie should simply give her interest in the cottage to her siblings. Peter shared Madeleine's position, reminding Natalie that he had two children in college and no available cash.

David and Natalie had very different opinions of the value of Natalie's interest, so I suggested that Natalie offer to split with

David the cost of an appraisal. The appraisal would be performed by a Member of the Appraisal Institute (appraisers with the MAI designation are highly qualified and their opinions respected). David was receptive to the idea, but wanted Natalie to accept "minority interest" and "marketability" discounts (such discounts often reduce the price of a fractional interest in property by twenty-five percent or more, reflecting a belief that outside buyers will pay proportionally less for shared property).

I reviewed a copy of Natalie's deed and confirmed that she and her siblings held title as "tenants in common." This inquiry was crucial: in some cases, siblings hold title as "joint tenants" or "joint tenants with right of survivorship." Full partition, the remedy I planned to recommend to Natalie, would not be available to her unless she and her siblings were tenants in common.

When Natalie asked about her options I didn't flip the lid off Pandora's box lightly — after all, the information I was about to impart would affect Natalie, her brothers, and her sister dramatically. Resisting the temptation to drag out the explanation for effect, I simply said "partition." This, I explained to Natalie, was the name of her legal right to force her brothers and sister to buy out her quarter interest in the cottage. If they didn't buy her out, then the court would order the cottage sold. She would receive a quarter of the net proceeds.

I warned Natalie that invoking partition would severely damage her relationship with her siblings. Natalie told me she was prepared for the hard feelings and that I should draft a demand letter to her brothers and sister. She wanted the letter to be civil, but firm. She assumed that David, an attorney, knew there was no defense to the action, but suspected he may not have explained to Madeleine and Peter what partition meant. Natalie also wanted Madeleine and Peter to know my legal fees would be charged against proceeds from the sale of the property (meaning each of the siblings would be contributing to the payment of my fees) and that properties sold through a court proceeding such as partition fetch a poor price — buyers understandably imposing a discount for the delay and uncertainty associated with a property in litigation.

Neither Natalie nor I expected the sale to take place. Instead, we felt the threat of partition would induce one or more of her siblings to buy out her share at a negotiated price.

The letter had the desired effect. Because David was an attorney he knew Natalie could force the sale of the cottage. He agreed to buy Natalie's interest for $148,000, which is $48,000 more than he initially offered, and about $50,000 less than Natalie believed her interest to be worth. The siblings also swapped items they'd been holding hostage from one another: David got his book on antique glass, Natalie got The Duck, a sentimental heirloom from the cottage. David finally provided her with the financial information she needed to file her 2006 income tax return. I concluded the sale several months after sending the demand letter. Natalie's parents would have been sad that the cottage was at the heart of a breakdown in the relationship among their children.

Afterward, Natalie told me that as the aunt with no children, she felt pressure to give her interest in the cottage to her nieces and nephews and sensed an implied threat of exclusion from the family if she forced a buyout. Natalie believed she would not have wanted to keep the cottage even if she had children. David said he viewed buyout as an advance on his kids' inheritance from Natalie, obviously presuming his children would be Natalie's heirs.

Natalie and her siblings are still not speaking.

Chapter 3

PLAN FOR THE BEST: COTTAGE SUCCESSION GOALS

Not only will a solid and clear cottage succession plan help ensure that your getaway stays in the family for generations, it also increases the chances for family harmony.

Using a limited liability company structure for your cottage creates a way to address most, if not all, areas of concern and conflict involving the cottage. If your plan states that it is not possible to sell the cottage without mutual agreement, for instance, heirs can't fight about whether it *should* be sold. If the heirs are *required* to contribute to ordinary cottage expenses in proportion to their actual use, then they can't fight about who pays what. If the heirs are *required* to buy out another heir and the price is determined by formula, then there is no need for an acrimonious negotiation or lawsuit over whether there will be a buyout and at what price.

The limited liability company structure used in cottage succession plans allows families to create rules that reflect their values, history, personalities, and hopes. These plans provide clear guidance to family members on issues that may arise in the course of owning the cottage. Some aspects of a cottage succession plan may be made rigid (nobody but descendants of founders may be owners), and other parts can be flexible (the schedule may be amended upon a vote of descendants who own a majority of the cottage LLC).

A good cottage succession plan should reflect the goals of the cottage founders and anticipate the wishes of cottage heirs. Let's look at these separately.

Founder Objectives

Some cottages owned by my clients have been in their families for more than 100 years. While others have acquired their cottages more recently, I cannot recall anyone saying to me, "I want my cottage to go to my children, but after that I don't care what happens." No, these clients envision generations of descendants cycling through the cottage. An unspoken hope, perhaps, is that their descendants will one day think fondly of the wise founders whose faded pictures adorn the walls.

The ultimate objective of founders is to keep the cottage in the family for multiple generations. I've identified three principal reasons for this:

+ Emotion: they and some (or all) of their descendants love the cottage more than its money equivalent.

+ Wealth accumulation: the cottage has been a terrific investment and the founders believe it will remain so.

+ Family unity: the founders believe the cottage will serve as a focal point for the family. As long as the cottage remains in the family, the founders expect the heirs will stay in touch with each other.

Founders appreciate better than heirs the obstacles to meeting this goal. They have heard horror stories about other families whose quest to keep the cottage failed. Families that have owned the cottage for a long time are likely to have experienced succession or sharing problems and will be drawn to the prospect of a plan that will avoid cottage traumas.

Founders expect a cottage succession plan to help overcome these obstacles, which include:

+ Ownership of an interest in the cottage passing into the hands of a child's spouse, whether as a consequence of the child's divorce or death.

+ The inability or unwillingness of a single heir to meet his financial obligations to the cottage.

+ The effect on the cottage of the bankruptcy of an heir, or the levy by a creditor of an heir on that heir's interest in the cottage.

+ The desire of an heir to cash out from the cottage.

+ Conflicts among heirs in how the cottage is operated, maintained, or improved.

+ Discord and even litigation among heirs (whether provoked by sibling rivalry, an heir's spouse, or an emotionally disturbed child).

+ The inability of the heirs, collectively, to afford to keep the cottage.

Traditional estate plans won't address these issues. LLC-based cottage succession plans should — and can.

Heir Concerns

Thoughtful heirs share many of the same concerns as founders. In addition, they have concerns arising from the knowledge that they must live with the cottage succession plan developed by the founders. These heir concerns are wrapped into one overriding worry: the founders will fail to do any cottage succession planning, leaving them to sort matters out as best they can.

A cottage succession plan can successfully address many heir concerns, which often are very specific, and involve day-to-day use, operation, and financing of the cottage.

The heirs, for instance, appreciate having a guaranteed right to use the cottage, but often worry more about the schedule. Will it be flexible enough to allow them use of the cottage when they have time off? What if one of the heirs tries to "squat" in the cottage? It happens.

Another concern is that some heirs won't be able to meet financial obligations to the cottage. Will some heirs (such as David Meade) have to bite their tongues and subsidize other heirs in the interest of family harmony?

Will each heir abide by the cottage rules concerning cleanliness? Although unusual in my experience, it is not impossible to imagine the results of a dysfunctional family member. Let's assume he persistently trashes the place, wrecks stuff, and commits other atrocities against family sensibilities. What could the heirs do in this case?

The heir who lives nearest the cottage justifiably worries that she will be expected to handle opening, closing, maintenance, and rental of the cottage. Will that heir be compensated? If so, how?

While the foregoing concerns are real, the "big one" is an heir's fear that their inheritance will be trapped in the cottage. Heirs realize that life is uncertain and worry that they will have no way to pull "their" money out of the cottage should they need it, or just want it.

A couple I represent purchased several hundred feet on a beautiful lake in the 1960s when land was inexpensive. Over time, the cottage increased in value to an amazing (to my clients) $1.3 million. The mother planned to leave the cottage equally to her three children along with a modest amount of cash. One might imagine how the children felt about their prospective inheritance — conflicted. Facing college or major medical expenses, would they need to sell a cottage share to siblings? What if siblings couldn't buy or refused to pay a fair price? Could one of them force a sale of the cottage and would it risk permanent family rupture? If she kept the cottage despite college or medical expenses, how would her spouse react? Would it give the appearance of putting the cottage and her siblings ahead of her husband and children? These and other heir concerns are very real. Cottages are sold to cover major medical expenses, families' relationships are strained when a cousin can't pay his share of cottage taxes, and a sister who lives close to the cottage may end up resenting the place because the burden of its upkeep is on her shoulders.

Shared Concerns

Then there is The Rabbit Problem. The following table (which would be familiar to population-growth experts, Thomas Malthus and Paul Ehrlich) shows how the number of potential users of the cottage — the "Alive" column — increases exponentially over time, so that in fifty years, a cottage could have fourteen owners, and in one hundred years, it could be split among fifty-six living relatives. This chart assumes each owner has two children and lives seventy-five years.

| | GENERATIONS → | | | | | | | |
	1st	2nd	3rd	4th	5th	6th	7th	**Alive**
0 years	2	2						**4**
25 years	2	2	4					**8**
50 years		2	4	8				**14**
75 years			4	8	16			**28**
100 years				8	16	32		**56**
125 years					16	32	64	**112**

The Rabbit Problem can jeopardize the cottage's future: the larger the number of owners holding title as tenants in common the more likely it is that one of them will file a partition suit to force a sale of the cottage. As bad as the chart looks, the reality is worse: it doesn't take into account spouses or friends of each of the owners.

Additionally, The Rabbit Problem sets the stage for family squabbles over use. Lake cottages are best in the summer. Ski lodges are best in the winter. People compete to use the cottage during specific weeks and holidays. Who gets the Fourth of July and who gets a rainy week in March? What happens when there are more than twelve owners and no one is guaranteed even a full week in high season? What then?

It is possible to address and resolve all founder and heir concerns — except one — by crafting an operating agreement under a limited liability company. This book will help you examine options for all these concerns.

The only issue that an operating agreement can't address, however, is heirs' overriding concern: the founders won't make a plan at all. And they're right to be concerned. Without a cottage plan, the possibility of family fractures and losing the cottage increases, like rabbits, with each generation.

Choosing the Right Path

Chapter 4

How a Plan
Helps Save the
Family Cottage

Sir William Blackstone, in his famous treatise on real estate law, said it best: "There is nothing which so generally strikes the imagination and enrages the affections of mankind, as the right of property...." When applied to the family cottage, he understated the problem.

When considering your cottage's future, it is vital to understand the differences between forms of ownership and the consequences of each. Persons may hold title to real estate such as a cottage either *directly* or *indirectly*. Real estate law, which developed through centuries of court cases, controls the rights and duties of *direct* owners. The rights and duties of *indirect* owners are established by the laws of trusts, partnerships, corporations, and limited liability companies, and not by real estate law.

Real estate law grants rights and imposes duties that frequently surprise cottage owners. These surprises put the cottage at risk.

A cottage succession plan relies upon indirect ownership because the real estate law (direct ownership) does not promote keeping the cottage in the family through multiple generations. Entity law (the laws of trusts, partnerships, corporations, and limited liability companies) has evolved over the years to accommodate complex realities of commerce, whereas real estate law has not changed greatly in hundreds of years. Entity law is extremely flexible and allows the creation of a cottage succession plan that is precisely tailored to the family wishes. *Transferring the cottage to a legal entity means that entity law, not real estate law, governs the relationship of the owners.*

This is not to say that a form of cottage succession plan cannot be created under real estate law. As I explain in Chapter 7, tenancy in common in conjunction with an ownership agreement is appropriate if the owners intend to sell the cottage in the near future, in which case a full-blown cottage succession plan may not be warranted. These agreements address current use issues (scheduling, payment of annual costs), and don't attempt to regulate the transfer of interests in the cottage (founder's death, spousal rights, or buy and sell provisions).

In upcoming chapters we'll explore in detail the nature, constraints, and possible situations resulting from direct ownership under real estate law, and contrast these with the outcome under indirect ownership arrangements, such as trusts, corporations and my preferred vehicle, the limited liability company.

To begin understanding crucial differences, let's explore some common cottage-related concerns and the outcomes under tenancy in common and a cottage succession plan that uses a limited liability company.

Concern: Ownership of an interest in the cottage passing into the hands of a child's spouse as a consequence of divorce or death.

UNDER REAL ESTATE LAW: Under the law of some states, the moment a man is married, his wife acquires an undivided one-third interest in the man's real property that is located in the state in which the couple resides. This right, called dower, confers upon the wife the right to inhabit the family cottage for the rest of her lifetime following her husband's death. For instance, if Andy and his brother, Bob, each owned a one-half of the family cottage as tenants in common in a dower state, on Andy's death Andy's widow automatically would have the right to share the cottage with Bob *even if Andy's estate plan left his entire interest in the cottage to Bob!*

WITH A COTTAGE SUCCESSION PLAN: A wife has no dower interest in her husband's interest in a cottage LLC. Although the divorce court has the power to award a spouse's interest in a cottage LLC to a non-heir spouse, the cottage operating agreement can treat the transfer as void, or can grant to the company (e.g. the rest of the family) the right to reacquire the transferred interest. This illustrates how the cottage LLC protects the family's interest in the cottage despite the divorce of a family member.

Concern: The inability or unwillingness of a single heir to meet financial obligations to the cottage.

Cottages require owners to pay money out every year for property taxes, maintenance, insurance, and improvements. The only time owner contributions would not be required is if the cottage is rented out frequently or if the founders set up an endowment for the cottage.

Under real estate law: Suppose four heirs own the cottage and each is required to contribute $3,000 per year for property taxes, maintenance, insurance, and improvements. If one of the heirs can't afford his share, or worse, if he can afford his share but refuses to pay, the only remedy available to the other heirs is to bring a lawsuit. Few heirs want to sue a relative, so they merely grouse, harbor resentment, and hope the circumstances will change.

With a cottage succession plan: A cottage succession plan may establish consequences for the heir's failure to pay. These consequences include the heir's loss of the right to use the cottage, a fine, an automatic reduction in the heir's ownership share, or any other sanction that the founders wish to impose. The delinquent heir is punished without a lawsuit.

◆

Concern: The effect on the cottage of an heir bankruptcy, or the levy on that heir's interest in the cottage by a creditor.

Creditors have powerful rights. One of these rights is to seize a debtor's assets. An interest in cottage real estate is such an asset.

Under real estate law: A creditor may seize the interest of an heir in the cottage. This interest can be used by the creditor or sold. A creditor that acquires ownership rights in a cottage may force the sale of the cottage to collect a debt.

With a cottage succession plan: A cottage succession plan can make creditor's attempts to seize an interest in the cottage an exercise in futility.

◆

Concern: An heir wants to cash out his share of the cottage.

Some heirs view a share of the cottage as a trapped inheritance. What happens if they want to cash out their interest?

UNDER REAL ESTATE LAW: In the absence of a cottage succession plan, most heirs hold title to the cottage in a form of ownership called tenancy in common. This form of ownership grants to each owner the right to force the sale of the cottage through a court proceeding known as partition. The remedy of partition is automatic. There is no defense. As a consequence, any heir at any time can make good on a demand to be cashed out of the cottage, regardless of the hardship this causes to the other owners.

WITH A COTTAGE SUCCESSION PLAN: A cottage succession plan prevents partition. The founders may choose to let an heir require the other heirs to cash him out, or the founders may refuse to confer this right. If the founders grant the right they may establish the price and terms of the buyout. *Prevent-* *ing partition, and providing for an orderly exit from the cottage by an heir, probably is the most important reason to establish a cottage succession plan.*

◆

Concern: Conflicts among heirs over how the cottage is operated, maintained, or improved.

Some heirs see the cottage as a time capsule. They relish the creak of the screen door, the musty smell, the faucet that works backwards. Others love the setting but wonder why anybody would put up with fifty-year-old plumbing and wiring, can't understand what is wrong with granite countertops, and love trash compactors.

Under real estate law: Heirs who co-own the cottage have a say in its operation and maintenance, but (to the surprise of many of my clients) *co-ownership does not mean majority rule.* A co-owner doesn't need anyone's permission to make a change to the cottage as long as those changes would not be viewed by a court as destructive or damaging.

Real estate law does not establish a standard of maintenance for the cottage, so if the heirs cannot agree upon the way a cottage is to be kept, its condition either drops to the lowest common denominator of care or the heir with the higher standard personally pays for the extra care.

With a cottage succession plan: Most cottage succession plans operate on a democratic principle. A majority of the heirs decide the standard of maintenance for the cottage. A majority of the heirs decide which improvements are to be made to the cottage. The majority may implement these decisions over the minority's objection. The majority also has the power to compel the dissenting heirs to contribute to the expense of the maintenance and improvements and may sanction the dissenting heirs who fail to make the required contributions.

The founders must exercise foresight in drafting a cottage succession plan so that a strong-willed (or well-heeled) heir does not oppress meeker, poorer, or more nostalgic heirs. Fortunately, a cottage succession plan is almost infinitely flexible. Protections for each heir may be drafted into the plan. By way of example, a cottage succession plan could allow a specified fraction of heirs to veto assessments for capital improvements. This fine-tuned control is impossible under real estate law ownership.

◆

Concern: Discord and even litigation among heirs (whether provoked by sibling rivalry, an heir's spouse, or an emotionally disturbed child).

Some families fight. And even in seemingly harmonious families it is difficult to predict how siblings will relate to one another once the parents are not around to mediate disputes.

UNDER REAL ESTATE LAW: If family disputes play out over the cottage (and for some reason they seem to), the likely outcome is an adversarial negotiation to buy out one of the heirs, a partition suit, or some other unpleasantness.

WITH A COTTAGE SUCCESSION PLAN: A cottage succession plan helps prevent disputes by establishing clear rules and standards and by imposing democratic principles upon the heirs. The disputes that remain may be resolved through the exercise of an heir's right to compel the other heirs to buy him out, or by compelling the disputants to submit the matter to a neutral mediator.

◆

Concern: The inability of the heirs, collectively, to afford to keep the cottage.

UNDER REAL ESTATE LAW: Many parents don't (or won't) think through whether their children actually can afford the gift of a cottage. I've seen the unhappy fallout. Occasionally the children acknowledge their inability to afford the cottage and agree to sell it. This ordinarily works out even if they must negotiate among themselves with respect to the sale price. A greater problem is when one child can afford the cottage and the others cannot, or if a child who cannot afford the cottage stubbornly refuses to let go. This results in litigation.

With a cottage succession plan: While no cottage succession plan can print money, it can offer a structured approach to the affordability problem. A cottage succession plan may be built around the proceeds of a life insurance policy if the founders are eligible for life insurance and able to afford substantial premiums. The policy death benefit may be directed to a fund — an endowment — that is invested by the heirs or a bank trust department. The income from the endowment may be dedicated to paying the expenses of keeping the cottage. The endowment's potential to work financial magic is discussed in Chapter 16.

If this solution is unavailable or unappealing, the founders should plan pragmatically. Perhaps one of their children is financially successful and the others are not. The estate plan of the parents could offer the wealthier child a right of first purchase on the cottage, the price to be its appraised value or some fraction of appraised value, as the parents deem fair. If the child exercises the right of first purchase, the cottage continues in the founder's line of descent but some of the children are cashed out. If the child does not exercise the right of first purchase, the personal representative or trustee of the deceased parent can be directed to sell the cottage and distribute the proceeds among the heirs. Centralizing the authority to handle the sale of the cottage in one person surely is better than distributing the cottage to all of the heirs and hoping that "things will just work out."

◆

A cottage succession plan is a tailored document. It reflects the values of the founders and seeks to balance the potentially divergent wishes of the heirs both living and unborn. While no document can achieve this perfectly, a cottage succession plan is superior to allowing the relationships of the heirs to be mediated by ancient real estate law principles. Because it is impossible for founders to see the future, the cottage succession plan is drafted to permit amendment. This allows the family to adapt to changing circumstances with the consent of a sufficient number of heirs. A cottage succession plan never will be perfect but it is always better than the alternative.

Chapter 5

No Plan? Then 600-Year-Old Law Controls the Cottage

When two or more people own cottage real estate directly they are said to have "concurrent ownership." For at least 600 years (and probably more than 800 years), the law has divided concurrent ownership into four principal types: *tenancy in common, joint tenancy* (and the related *joint tenancy with right of survivorship*), and *tenancy by the entireties*. The characteristics of these "estates in land" have confused generations of law students and attorneys, but are so important to cottage succession planning that it is worth taking the effort to understand the basic principles.

The language in the first paragraph of your deed is crucial. So that you understand the nature of your current title, I suggest you locate a copy of the most recent deed to your cottage and refer to it as we discuss your title to the cottage.

Tenancy in Common

Tenancy in common is the most common form of joint ownership, so let's explore this kind of relationship first.

A "tenancy in common" is established when property is transferred in the following form:

From A to B and C

or

From A to B and C as tenants in common

or

**From A to B and C as tenants in common
and not as joint tenants**

A tenancy in common is the usual way children receive title to the cottage when they inherit it from their parents. Each child is referred to as a "tenant in common." Collectively the children are "tenants in common." The words "tenant" and "tenancy" refer to the current right to use the property and do not imply a rental arrangement (a point of confusion for many first-year law students).

The governing principles of tenancy in common, which I present in this chapter as "rules," are described below. They were distilled by me from leading treatises on real property law. Although labeling a common law doctrine as a "rule" implies an exactness that is not found in the case law, my rules are a fair statement of the law governing the relationship of tenants in common.

If you do not have a cottage plan it is highly likely the tenancy in common rules will govern your cottage. If you are a parent who is thinking of passing a cottage on to your children in a way that results in their owning it as tenants in common, you should know what this form of ownership will mean to your children. This section also will educate you about your rights and responsibilities if you are a sibling or a cousin who owns a share of your cottage as a tenant in common.

The Smith Family

We'll use a fictional family, the Smiths, to illustrate the rules of tenancy in common. Assume that Mom and Dad Smith transfer the family cottage — a lodge with 150 feet of shoreline — to their children, Andy, Bob, and Carol, as tenants in common.

Andy, fifty-three, has three sons, and is the oldest child. He lives 400 miles from the cottage and owns a carpet and tile business, which is struggling. Bob, fifty-one, the middle child, is single, childless, affluent, and frequently posted overseas by his employer, a multinational corporation. At forty-eight, Carol is the baby of the family. She moved to the resort community near the cottage and married Tom, a "local." Carol and Tom have two children and are comfortable but have little discretionary income. The three siblings love the cottage equally. Let's examine how the rules of tenancy in common may affect the Smiths.

Rule 1: Each tenant in common has a right of partition.

EXAMPLE 1: Even though Andy depleted his life savings propping up the carpet and tile business, it finally fails. Andy is nearly broke, his share of the cottage the last valuable asset he possesses. With utmost reluctance, he decides he cannot afford his share of the cottage any longer and asks Bob and Carol to buy him out. They refuse.

> CONSEQUENCE: Andy consults with a real estate attorney. The attorney describes his right of partition. Andy, feeling he is out of options, files suit. The judge rules that the cottage cannot be divided physically into three equal parts and orders the cottage sold. Bob and Carol are stunned.

Partition, a drastic remedy, reduces the status of the cottage from a sacred family retreat to a mere economic asset. It elevates the *economic* interest of one cottage owner over the *emotional* and *sentimental* interests that other owners may have in the cottage. To some family members, however, no amount of money would compensate them for the loss of the cottage. To these owners it is literally priceless.

The advocate for partition would argue:

+ A co-owner may prevent the sale of the cottage simply by paying fair market value to the owner who no longer wishes to own a share. To the argument that "I can't afford to buy you out," the proponent of partition is often heard to say, "That isn't my fault."

+ Partition is a 600-year-old remedy, so legal Darwinism suggests that it is a good thing.

+ We cannot place a value on sentiment, therefore, we must ignore it.

+ Partition is economically efficient because it increases the overall wealth of society and therefore adds to the total social good.

EXAMPLE 2: Assume siblings Harold and Sally own a cottage as tenants in common, that Harold's liquid net worth is $50,000 and Sally's is $200,000. Sally decides she wants the cottage to herself and files a partition suit. Harold bids everything in his savings and checking accounts: $50,000. Sally bids $50,001 and acquires Harold's share of the cottage. Is this a fair result?

Harold would argue that he proved his love for the cottage by offering to pay his *entire liquid net worth* for the cottage. Sally only bid twenty-five percent of her net worth. Some have argued that a fair partition method would take into account the intensity of a bidder's feelings for property (as measured by the percentage of the bidder's net worth offered to acquire the asset) rather than merely its monetary value to determine who wins the asset in a partition sale. While an interesting theory, this approach is not the law now and is not likely to be the law anytime soon.

The right of partition described in this rule is not absolute. A cottage succession plan may prevent exercise of the right of partition while still allowing a family member to make a graceful exit from ownership. The method for achieving this (the "put option") is described in Chapter 11.

Rule 2: Each tenant in common owns an "undivided interest" in the cottage.

EXAMPLE 1: Returning to the Smith family, Andy and Carol each insist on the right to use the cottage for the first two weeks of July.

> CONSEQUENCE: Andy owns one-third of the entire property; Bob owns one-third of the entire property; Carol owns one-third of the entire property. None of them has the right to exclude a co-owner. In other words, it is not as if any sibling can exclude the others from "his" fifty feet. Under common law neither Andy nor Carol has a clear right to the first two weeks of July. Other than partition there is no resolution to the problem if they cannot agree.

EXAMPLE 2: Assume that Mom and Dad decided to give Andy sixty percent of the cottage, Bob thirty percent of the cottage, and Carol ten percent of the cottage.

> CONSEQUENCE: Andy, Bob, and Carol have the simultaneous right to use the cottage whenever they want. Andy does not have the right to *exclusive* use of the property sixty percent of

the time. Andy does, however, have to pay sixty percent of cottage expenses, and will receive sixty percent of the proceeds if the cottage is sold. Until the cottage is sold Andy is subsidizing its use by Bob and Carol.

This example illustrates the surprising, and probably unintended, result of transferring a cottage to children in unequal shares as tenants in common. A child with a one percent interest in the cottage has use rights equal to the child with a ninety-nine percent interest! Each, however, must pay for cottage expense in proportion to his ownership.

EXAMPLE 3: There is only room for one boat at the dock. Bob ties his Gar Wood to the dock for the entire summer so the boat is ready when he visits. Andy wants to use the dock for a rented pontoon boat during his vacation. Who gets to use the dock?

CONSEQUENCE: Bob must pay fair market rent for the dock if his exclusive use deprives Andy of the right to use the dock.

EXAMPLE 4: Bob gets there first, claims squatter's rights and forces Andy to moor the pontoon boat out in the lake. Andy has to swim to the boat. The more he thinks about it, the madder Andy gets. In retaliation Andy paints the cottage purple.

CONSEQUENCE: Andy has the right to the dock, but unless he sets the Gar Wood adrift, Bob's equal right to the dock blocks Andy's use. Bob and Carol have no legal basis for challenging Andy's choice of paint color.

EXAMPLE 5: Bob wants to expand and modernize the cottage at his expense.

CONSEQUENCE: Bob may do so over the objection of his siblings. The project would be viewed by a court as benefiting the cottage so Andy and Carol do not have a legal basis for objecting to the changes made by Bob.

EXAMPLE 6: Let's assume Andy needs cash (a big carpet shipment is coming in C.O.D.). Andy's bank grudgingly makes the loan, but insists on taking security in all of Andy's business assets, a second mortgage on his house, *and* a mortgage on his interest in the cottage.

CONSEQUENCE: May Andy grant a mortgage on his interest? Absolutely. A tenant in common's separate interest in the cottage may be pledged as security for debt. And if Andy doesn't pay the loan off, the lender may foreclose his interest in the cottage by following the statutory procedure. The theoretical consequence (I have not seen this example in my practice) is that a stranger would wind up with Andy's interest in the cottage ("Excuse me, where do you keep the towels?"). Andy is within his rights to grant the mortgage. Neither Bob nor Carol can interfere with the loan.

Rule 3: A tenant in common has the right to transfer his interest to any person at any time.

EXAMPLE 1: Andy gives his one-third interest in the cottage to the Salvation Army over the objections of Bob and Carol.

Or, Andy gives his one-third interest in the cottage to his delinquent, pyromaniac son, Freddie.

Or, Andy sells his interest to Carol, even though he had always told Bob that Bob would have the first right to purchase the interest.

CONSEQUENCE: Andy has acted within his rights in each case. No tenant in common can prevent his co-tenant from disposing of his interest to absentees or irresponsible persons. Bob and Carol could share ownership of the cottage with the Salvation Army or Freddie. In the third example, Carol will own two-thirds of the cottage and bear two-thirds of its expenses. She will not, however, be guaranteed two-thirds of its use (see Rule 2).

EXAMPLE 2: Andy dies suddenly. Because Andy wanted to keep the cottage in the family and felt that his children would never be able to afford the costs of his share, Andy's last will and testament specified that his interest in the cottage would be given to Bob and Carol at his death.

CONSEQUENCE: If Andy and his wife lived in a state that recognized the dower interest of a woman, Andy's wife could retain a partial interest in the cottage notwithstanding Andy's last will and testament. Andy's surviving wife would have the right to use the cottage, or could force its sale in a partition action.

Rule 4: A tenant in common does not owe rent to the other owners for using the cottage.

EXAMPLE 1: Bob lost his job. He loves the cottage but is short of funds. Bob has nowhere to stay other than the cottage and decides to set up camp there. Bob lives in the cottage for about nine months making it uncomfortable for the others to use the cottage, even though it has four bedrooms.

Consequence: Andy and Carol have no right to collect rent from Bob despite his disproportionate use of the cottage. Sole possession by one tenant is not presumed to be adverse to the rights of other co-tenants.

Example 2: Same facts, except Bob threatens his siblings with bodily harm if they try to use the cottage.

Consequence: Bob may have "ousted" Andy and Carol. If so, Bob owes them rent.

Example 3: Same facts, except the cottage has only one bedroom, which prevents Andy and Carol from using the cottage at all until Bob leaves.

Consequence: Bob would owe Andy and Carol rent under the laws of most states.

Rule 5: A tenant in common may rent out the cottage to third parties without the consent of the other owners.

This rule of law can pose a real problem. Wealthier children may not want strangers using the cottage, while the poorer children may not be able to afford their cottage assessment without renting out their weeks from time to time.

Example 1: The negative cash flow of the cottage is $15,000 per year, so Andy, Bob, and Carol each contribute $5,000 annually. By prior agreement each is entitled to use the cottage for a month. Bob's month is July. Bob is sent to Japan for a two-year assignment. Bob announces that he is renting his month to his fraternity buddy, Ed. Andy and Carol, remembering with displeasure Ed's last visit, object to Bob's plan.

CONSEQUENCE: Bob may rent the cottage to Ed for the month of July over Andy and Carol's objection.

EXAMPLE 2: Bob's friend Frank needs a place to store his boat. Flush with power, Bob reasons that if he can rent the cottage to Ed for July, he also can rent the garage to Frank. He does so.

CONSEQUENCE: Because the storage lease impermissibly prevents Andy and Carol from using the garage for the entire year Andy and Carol may terminate the lease or force Bob to share the rent paid by Frank.

Rule 6: A tenant in common is not required to compensate another tenant for services associated with management of the cottage.

EXAMPLE: Carol lives in a resort community near the cottage. Andy and Bob live far away. The family needs to rent the cottage for six weeks each year to provide funds to pay the property tax. Carol locates tenants by running ads in the newspaper, interviews the tenants, collects the damage deposits, arranges to have the cottage clean when the tenants arrive, responds to tenant's concerns, and inspects the cottage after each group of tenants departs. Carol ensures proper records are kept and tax filings made, although sometimes Bob helps. Carol has done this for many years. Sometimes she feels put upon but recognizes that, because she is the closest to the cottage, she is the logical sibling to perform this function.

CONSEQUENCE: Without an agreement, Andy and Bob are not obligated to compensate Carol for her extra work.

A short history of tenancy in common in America

In 1776, unless otherwise specified, American law assumed that new co-owners of property were joint tenants with survivorship rights, a relationship that disinherits the spouse and children of the first co-owner to die. Soon after Independence, however, states began to reverse this presumption. North Carolina called joint tenancy a "manifest injustice" to families because it resulted in complete disinheritance of branches of a family.

Today all fifty states treat property transferred to two or more unmarried people as tenants in common unless otherwise specified in the deed or conveyancing document.

Rule 7: A tenant in common is not entitled to reimbursement for improvements or repairs to the cottage (unless the repairs are necessary to preserve the cottage).

EXAMPLE 1: The carpet in the living room of the cottage is soiled and smells like Skipper, Andy's old mutt. Carol has been after her brothers for years to replace the carpet. They cannot understand what Carol is so riled up about; after all, this is a cottage, not a palace. In frustration, Carol orders new carpet and has it installed at her expense.

CONSEQUENCE: Carol is not entitled to reimbursement for two reasons: 1) the carpet is not a capital improvement; and 2) Carol's brothers did not ask her to install the carpet.

EXAMPLE 2: The cottage has not been painted in ten years. There is little money in the kitty, and neither brother is willing to chip in to hire a painter. Carol and her son, David, devote their entire summer to repainting the cottage. When the next property tax bill comes due, Carol asks her brothers to waive her share of the contribution to reward her efforts. Her brothers refuse, responding to Carol's complaints of overwork by pointing out that she gets to use the cottage more often than they do. Carol huffs that she is too busy with maintenance to enjoy her time at the cottage.

> CONSEQUENCE: Carol and David threaten to take the brothers to small claims court to claim compensation for their labor and the cost of the paint. Their suit will succeed only if they can prove to the judge that the painting was necessary to preserve the cottage. If the painting was done for aesthetic reasons (Carol didn't like the color), they will not be entitled to compensation. The judge also might deny compensation because, due to Carol's extra use of the cottage, charging the brothers would be unfair.

EXAMPLE 3: The cottage roof and septic system are failing. Bob suggests they mortgage the cottage for $30,000 to pay for these much-needed repairs. Andy and Carol refuse, fearing Bob is trying to squeeze them out of the cottage in some way ("besides, the roof isn't that bad"). Frustrated, Bob hires the contractors anyway and has the work done.

> CONSEQUENCE: Bob is entitled to reimbursement because the improvements were required to preserve the cottage. Bob may have to sue his siblings to collect. If, however, Bob was the sole user of the cottage for a long period, the court might reduce the amount Bob is owed by the reasonable rental value of his use of the cottage.

Rule 8: A tenant in common who pays a disproportionate share of expenses is not necessarily entitled to reimbursement.

EXAMPLE 1: For the last five years Bob has paid all expenses of keeping the cottage. Bob demands reimbursement.

> CONSEQUENCE: Bob is entitled to reimbursement for property taxes. It is less clear that Bob will succeed in collecting a share of the mortgage or insurance payments he made on his siblings' behalf. Bob will have to sue them to collect if Andy and Carol do not volunteer the money. Bob's right to reimbursement is not automatic. If, for instance, Bob made disproportionate use of the cottage during the five-year period, a judge might deny Bob's demand on the grounds that his extra use of the cottage was sufficient compensation.

EXAMPLE 2: The assessor sent a tax bill for one-third of the cottage taxes to Andy, another tax bill for one-third of the cottage taxes to Bob, and a third bill for the balance of the cottage taxes to Carol. Carol fails to pay her property tax bill and neglects to tell her brothers. They learn about it when Carol's interest is put up for tax sale. Andy and Bob pay the back taxes, penalties, and interest.

> CONSEQUENCE: If Carol refuses to reimburse Andy and Bob, the brothers' only recourse is to sue Carol for reimbursement. If Andy and Bob didn't learn of Carol's neglect, a stranger could purchase the interest at the tax sale and acquire Carol's one-third interest in the cottage. Some states would have required the assessor to give notice to Andy and Bob, other states would not.

Rule 9: A tenant in common has only limited duties to the other tenants in common.

EXAMPLE: Bob handles the homeowner's insurance. He insures his one-third share, but doesn't buy insurance for Andy or Carol's interest in the cottage. The cottage burns down. Bob collects from his insurance company, but Andy and Carol receive nothing.

CONSEQUENCE: Provided Bob didn't promise Andy or Carol that he would take care of the insurance on their behalf, neither Andy nor Carol have a claim against Bob because he has no duty to insure their interests in the cottage.

Chapter 6

OTHER ANIMALS
IN THE
PROPERTY LAW ZOO

If your deed says something other than "tenants in common," your cottage may fall under one of the other common law categories of real estate ownership that are examined here. As with tenancy in common, these categories of ownership can make your cottage vulnerable to partition (a forced sale) and family feuds.

We'll examine joint tenancy, joint tenancy with rights of survivorship, tenancy with rights of survivorship, tenancy by the entireties, and community property.

Joint Tenancy

The form of title called "joint tenancy" is established when property is deeded this way:

From A to B and C as joint tenants
or
From A to B, C, D, and E as joint tenants

The nine rules described in Chapter 5 also apply to joint tenants. The unique feature of joint tenancy is that it is a winner-takes-all longevity contest. If Bob and Carol own the property as joint tenants, at Bob's death, Carol becomes the sole owner of the property. If Carol dies first, Bob becomes the sole owner of the property. Neither survivor must take any further action to gain ownership of the entire property. It happens automatically. In the second example the last survivor of B, C, D, and E will own the entire property.

Many owners do not understand the implications of this form of ownership. In my practice I have seen children devastated when they learn their parent's share of a cottage simply disappeared and that their aunt or uncle now is the sole owner of the cottage.

EXAMPLE 1: Mom and Dad Smith deed the cottage to Andy, Bob, and Carol as joint tenants. Andy and Bob die.

CONSEQUENCE: Carol becomes the sole owner of the cottage. Andy's children receive no interest in the cottage (Bob had no children).

EXAMPLE 2: Mom and Dad deed the cottage to Andy, Bob, and Carol as joint tenants. Andy and Bob die. Andy's will leaves his one-third interest in the cottage to his three children.

CONSEQUENCE: Carol becomes the sole owner of the cottage. *Andy's children still receive no interest in the cottage.* Andy's interest in the cottage terminated automatically at his death, and so could not pass to his probate estate to be distributed to his children. This is a fairly common result and an unhappy surprise to those people who believe their last will and testament is the final word on disposition of their property.

EXAMPLE 3: Mom and Dad deed the cottage to Andy, Bob, and Carol as joint tenants. Andy deeds his one-third interest in the cottage to his three children. Bob subsequently dies.

CONSEQUENCE: Andy's action severs his interest as a joint tenant. His children share a one-third tenancy in common with Bob and Carol, who — as a unit — hold the other two-thirds of the tenancy in common interest. Within the unit, however, *Bob and Carol remain joint tenants.* While Bob is alive, the tenancy in common is shared, as to one-ninth by each of Andy's children and as to two-thirds by Bob and Carol. Carol acquires Bob's interest at Bob's death by virtue of their joint tenancy, and so will own two-thirds of the property as tenants in common with Andy's three children (who retain their individual one-ninth interests).

EXAMPLE 4: Mom and Dad deed the cottage to Andy, Bob, and Carol as joint tenants. Andy needs money and asks Bob and Carol to buy his share. They refuse. He brings an action for partition.

CONSEQUENCE: The court will grant Andy's request for partition and order the property sold.

EXAMPLE 5: Carol develops a terminal disease and asks her lawyer to update her estate plan. The lawyer determines the cottage is owned in joint tenancy. Carol's lawyer tells her that if she dies before Andy and Bob her children cannot inherit her share of the cottage.

CONSEQUENCE: Carol asks her brothers to buy out her share of the cottage. They talk to their own lawyers and realize if they do nothing Carol's death will terminate her interest in the cottage. They make a ridiculously low offer to Carol for her interest in the cottage. Carol refuses the offer, and then exercises her right of transfer (Rule 3) by deeding her one-third interest in the cottage to her children. This severs the joint tenancy only as to Carol's one-third interest. When Carol dies, Andy and Bob — as a unit — are joint tenants as to their two-thirds interest, and Carol's two children each own a one-sixth interest in the cottage as tenants in common. Each of Carol's children has the full right to use the cottage (Rule 2). Would Andy and Bob have made a more generous offer to Carol had they anticipated that they will have to share the cottage with two people instead of one?

Joint Tenancy with Right of Survivorship

Joint tenancy *with right of survivorship* (JTWROS) is a special form of joint tenancy. It is created by a deed in any of the following forms:

From A to B and C and to the survivor of them

or

From A to B and C or the survivor of them

or

From A to B and C with right of survivorship

or

From A to B and C as joint tenants with full rights of survivorship

or

**From A to B and C as joint tenants with right of survivorship
and not as tenants in common**

The type of JTWROS described in this section exists in only a few states, among them Michigan. Unlike a standard joint tenancy, which may be terminated by *any* joint tenant, "indestructible JTWROS" cannot be terminated without the consent of *all* joint tenants.

People use joint tenancy and JTWROS to bypass probate because these forms of ownership result in the automatic termination of the interest of the deceased owner, leaving the survivors alone in title. Like "regular" joint tenancy, significant complications can arise from JTWROS, such as inadvertently disinheriting whole branches of a family.

Normally I counsel parents not to deed property to their children JTWROS during the parents' lifetime. The reason is that JTWROS gives children a stake in their parents' property during their parents' lifetimes. If, for instance, the parent transfers a cottage to his children and himself using JTWROS, and the parent dies first (the normal order of things), then the parent has succeeded in avoiding probate of the cottage. The children then own the cottage JTWROS. But what if the children can't get along? JTWROS prevents a full partition of their interests! What if the parent decides to sell the cottage to finance a stay in assisted living and the child won't sign the listing agreement or deed? The property remains unsold.

Despite all these drawbacks, there remains a potential use for JTWROS in cottage succession planning. Assume that parents know their children can't get along, but don't have the resources or desire to prepare a cottage succession plan. The parents could deed the cottage to their children and themselves as JTWROS. The children will hold title to the cottage as JTWROS after the parents die. Neither the children nor a court can end their mutual entanglement. On the one hand this can result in an unfixable mess. On the other it forces the children to share the cottage.

Witness some possible examples with JTWROS:

EXAMPLE 1: Mom and Dad deed the cottage to Andy, Bob, and Carol as JTWROS. Andy and Bob die.

CONSEQUENCE: Carol becomes the sole owner of the cottage. Andy's children receive no interest in the cottage. (Bob had no children.)

EXAMPLE 2: Mom and Dad deed the cottage to Andy, Bob, and Carol as JTWROS. Andy and Bob die. Andy's last will and testament left his one-third interest in the cottage to his three children.

CONSEQUENCE: Carol becomes the sole owner of the cottage. Andy's children still receive no interest in the cottage. Andy's interest in the cottage terminated automatically at his death and could not pass to his probate estate to be distributed to his children.

EXAMPLE 3: Mom and Dad deed the cottage to Andy, Bob, and Carol as JTWROS. Andy deeds his one-third interest in the cottage to his three children. Bob subsequently dies.

CONSEQUENCE: Bob's interest disappears at his death. Although Andy deeded his interest to his children, their ability to become the sole owner of the property depends upon Andy's outliving Carol. The deed conferred upon Andy's children the right to use the cottage during Andy's lifetime. If Andy outlives Carol, Andy's children own the entire cottage free of any claim of interest by Carol's children. If Carol outlives Andy, the rights of Andy's children terminate instantly. Carol will own 100 percent of the cottage and may do with it as she pleases.

EXAMPLE 4: Mom and Dad deed the cottage to Andy, Bob, and Carol as JTWROS. Andy needs money and brings an action for partition.

> CONSEQUENCE: The court may order a division and sale of the rights of Andy, Bob, and Carol to use the cottage during their lifetimes but may not alter the outcome of the longevity contest. The sibling who lives the longest will become the sole owner of the cottage. Andy will receive money from the sale of his life interest (somebody surely would gamble a little money to have the right to a share of the cottage during Andy's lifetime), but he will not receive one-third of the value of the cottage due to the uncertain outcome of the longevity contest.

EXAMPLE 5: Mom and Dad deed the cottage to Andy, Bob, and Carol as JTWROS. Andy's wife, Alice, and Carol hate each other. Andy and Carol have agreed to buy out Bob. Alice, a lawyer, tells Carol she won't allow Andy to close the deal unless the family switches to tenancy in common. Carol refuses based upon her fear that Alice might divorce Andy, acquire his interest in the cottage, and bring a partition action.

> CONSEQUENCE: The sale to Bob doesn't go through. Carol is relieved in a way, as JTWROS is protecting the cottage from Alice's machinations. Carol knows that even if Andy and Alice divorce, Andy won't lose his share of the cottage. Carol assumes that Andy and she will figure it out someday.

Tenancy by the Entireties

Tenancy by the entireties is a special form of ownership that exists in thirty-one states. It may be viewed as a JTWROS between husband and wife. In fact, the only people who may hold property as tenants by the entireties are husband and wife. A tenancy by the entireties is created by a deed in this form:

From A to B and C, as husband and wife

The legal fiction underpinning tenancy by the entirety is that the husband and wife are one person. While we all know couples like this, we also know couples for which this would be the least appropriate description!

The key feature of tenancy by the entireties is that, unlike a standard joint tenancy (which may be converted to a tenancy in common by the act of any owner), neither husband nor wife may destroy this estate without the consent of the other.

Tenancy by the entireties has been criticized as an anachronistic and sexist artifact of the feudal era because its benefits are not available to unmarried couples (straight or gay). The American Bar Association and many commentators have criticized this form of ownership or called for its abolition.

EXAMPLE: Granddad deeds the property to Mom and Dad as husband and wife. Mom thinks they should establish a cottage succession plan. Dad disagrees.

CONSEQUENCE: Neither parent acting alone may deed property in connection with the establishment of a cottage succession plan. The surviving parent, however, may do so.

Community Property

Community property is a property ownership system used only in Arizona, California, Idaho, Louisiana, Nevada, New Mexico, Texas, Washington, and Wisconsin. The mobility of our society means that many individuals will, at some point in their marriage, live in one of these states. If they do, community property laws will affect their interests in property such as a cottage even after they have moved out of the community property state.

The community property system treats a married couple as an economic partnership. The husband and the wife each are considered to have contributed equally to the partnership so property acquired during their marriage ("community property") is deemed to be owned equally by each spouse. If they divorce, each of the couple's assets is placed into one of three categories: *his* separate property, *her* separate property, and *their* community property. A spouse's separate property includes assets owned by a spouse before the marriage and assets acquired by a spouse during the marriage through gift or inheritance. The divorcing spouse may keep his or her separate property. The remaining community property is divided equally between the divorcing spouses.

A cottage acquired by a married couple who reside in a community property state is community property (assuming it was acquired with community assets). A cottage inherited by one of these spouses during their marriage, however, remains the separate property of the inheriting spouse, and may be disposed of as the inheriting spouse sees fit. The inheriting spouse, for example, could give the cottage to the couple's children, not to the other spouse.

States vary in the degree to which the surviving spouse may control the deceased spouse's interest in community property. For instance, community property passes to the spouse if a resident of California, Idaho, Nevada, New Mexico, and Washington dies without a last will and testament, but community property of a resident of Louisiana, Texas, or Wisconsin who dies without a last will and testament passes to his statutory heirs.

Example 1: Frank is married to Georgina. They reside in California. Frank has three children from his first marriage: Huey, Dewey, and Louie. Frank and Georgina also have a son, Donald, from their marriage. Frank inherits a share of his parents' New Hampshire cottage. Frank's last will and testament gives his interest in the cottage to his four children.

> **Consequence:** Frank may cut Georgina out of his estate plan. His interest in the cottage is his separate property because he acquired it as a gift from his parents.

Example 2: Same facts, except Frank and Georgina used community funds to rehab the cottage.

> **Consequence:** Georgina has some community property interest in the cottage. Georgina is entitled to a one-half share of the community property of the cottage at Frank's death. The balance, Frank's separate property, passes to Huey, Dewey, and Louie. Georgina may bring an action for partition. In addition, some states would give Georgina the right to manage the property during the administration of Frank's estate.

The lesson here is that community property laws may affect your interest in a cottage even if you no longer live in one of the nine community property states. Spouses who may have a community property interest in a cottage or the money used to buy or improve a cottage should consult with a lawyer in the community property state to determine the extent to which the *membership interest* in the cottage entity retains its community property character.

Chapter 7

Short-Term Solutions

The preceding sections suggest that cottage owners should avoid traditional direct real estate ownership. While generally true, in a few special cases real estate law, used properly, provides a simple solution to a complex problem. This chapter describes these solutions.

Using Life Estates

Common law recognized the usefulness of allowing a person the right to use a piece of real property for the duration of that person's life, while at the same time denying that person the right to confer rights in that property after the person's death. On the following pages I describe how I have used this right, called a "life estate," in cottage planning.

A life estate is created by deed in the following form:

From B to A and C, reserving to B a life estate

A and C, who hold a remainder interest in the property, are the **remaindermen**, and B, who holds a life estate in the property, is the **life tenant**. B pays a share of the property taxes and maintenance and may make improvements to the cottage (unless the deed or separate agreement provides otherwise). B is not obligated to insure the cottage, but may do so to the extent of his interest. When B dies (or if there is more than one life tenant, when the last one dies), full ownership of the cottage passes to A and C automatically (no need for probate administration).

Example 1: This time Mom and Dad Smith passed the cottage on to Andy, Bob, and Carol, who own it as tenants in common. Bob has no children and will remain childless. Bob wants the right to use the cottage for the balance of his lifetime, a right Andy and Carol are happy to acknowledge. Andy and Carol each have children. They worry, however, that Bob might marry and give his interest in the cottage to his new wife.

They propose a deal to Bob. If Bob will give up his remainder interest in the cottage, Andy and Carol will pick up cottage expenses for the rest of Bob's lifetime. Bob deeds his interest in the cottage to Andy and Carol, reserving a life estate to himself. A separate agreement states that all cottage expenses will be paid by Andy and Carol.

> **Consequence:** Andy, Bob, and Carol share use of the cottage during their lifetimes. Andy and Carol are assured they will be the sole owners of the cottage at Bob's death. Bob knows his right to use the cottage cannot be taken away even if Andy and Carol sell the cottage.

Caution: A plan such as this should not be undertaken lightly. Bob's life estate will interfere with the sale of the cottage because few buyers would be willing to let Bob occupy their acquisition for the rest of his lifetime. Nevertheless, in the right circumstance, especially for a family that does not want a full-blown cottage succession plan, the life estate is an elegantly simple solution.

The life estate does not solve all of the family's problems, however. Athough they have segregated Bob's interest, Andy and Carol continue to own the cottage as tenants in common and remain exposed to the problems described in Chapter 5. They can solve these problems with a cottage LLC.

EXAMPLE 2: Same facts as Example 1. A buyer approaches Andy and Carol with an offer of $800,000 — an excellent price. They would love to accept it, but now are stuck with Bob's life estate.

CONSEQUENCE: Bob doesn't want to be difficult. For the right price he would agree to give up his life estate in the cottage. He wonders what a fair price would be for his interest. Bob's accountant informs him the Internal Revenue Service publishes a table that values life interests based upon mortality tables. Bob is sixty-five at the time of the offer. The IRS factor for a sixty-five-year-old is 0.56195. Multiplying this factor by the offered price of $800,000 and then dividing by three (recall that Bob only had a one-third interest in the cottage to begin with) values Bob's life estate at $149,853. Bob agrees to this price. Andy, Bob, and Carol deed the cottage to the buyer. Andy and Carol each receive sales proceeds of $325,073; Bob keeps the remaining $149,853. Had Bob been forty-five at the time of the offer, the IRS factor would have been 0.79356 and he would have pocketed $211,616.

The Ownership Agreement

The purpose of a cottage succession plan is to keep a cottage in the family for a long time. I explain in subsequent chapters why the limited liability company is the right entity to use for this purpose.

How should a family (or unrelated owners) plan if they do not intend to keep their cottage indefinitely, but rightfully fear the consequences of direct real estate ownership? An interim solution might be for the cottage owners to enter into a contract that I call an "ownership agreement."

Among the reasons people may choose an ownership agreement: they expect to sell the cottage in the near future; they cannot come to agreement on enough of the LLC items to implement one; or they are unable to afford a cottage LLC, which, because it attempts to address all cottage issues, requires more attorney time for consultations and drafting, hence costs more to implement.

Although an ownership agreement, which is not effective without the signature of each owner, is only a partial solution to cottage issues, it is certainly better than having no agreement at all. The essential elements of an ownership agreement are:

+ Each owner must waive his right of partition.

+ Agreement regarding sharing use of the cottage (e.g. scheduling).

+ Agreement regarding sharing expenses of the cottage.

+ Agreement that determines how decisions are made (which decisions may be made by a simple majority? which decisions require unanimous agreement?).

Optional clauses in an ownership agreement include:

+ Transfer restrictions.

+ Reciprocal rights of first purchase.

+ Prohibitions upon mortgaging one's interest.

An ownership agreement can prevent partition of the cottage, at least for a reasonable amount of time and provided circumstances haven't changed since the agreement was signed. Because of its limited duration, the ownership agreement is not as effective for multi-generation cottage planning as are limited liability companies, trusts, and corporations.

Cottage Plans in Action

Chapter 8

CHOOSE THE RIGHT LEGAL ENTITY FOR YOUR COTTAGE

Direct ownership of a cottage under real estate law means a precarious future for your cottage and family. But there is an alternative. Indirect ownership of the cottage — through a trust, partnership, corporation, or limited liability company — allows owners to replace real estate doctrines with laws intended largely for business entities. This enables you to create an arrangement specifically tailored to your family's wishes. *You* get to decide how the cottage will be operated; *you* get to determine how it will be financed; and, most importantly, *you* get to say how the cottage will pass from generation to generation.

Most forms of indirect ownership use legal entities. The distinction between direct and indirect ownership of a cottage is crucial.

A key benefit of indirect ownership through a legal entity is that the right entity can shield you, the cottage owner, from personal liability to a person who is injured at the cottage. Assume your cottage is rented out and due to negligent heating system maintenance the renters are killed by carbon monoxide. If you own the cottage under real estate law, through general partnership, or you are the trustee of a revocable living trust that owns the cottage, all of your personal assets can be taken to pay the grieving relatives. If, instead, the cottage is owned by a corporation, limited partnership, or limited liability company, the lawyer for the grieving relatives may take the cottage property, but cannot make a claim against your home, your brokerage account, and your other personal assets.

Legal entities are created by filing organizational documents with a state office (typically the "Department of Corporations" or a division of the Secretary of State's office). The documents filed may be in the state where the cottage is located or in another state with more favorable laws.

Let's examine the different forms of indirect ownership for cottages:

Trusts and General Partnerships

Trusts and general partnerships are not separate legal entities. No document is filed with the state regulators to establish either and neither form provides a liability shield.

While some attorneys implement cottage plans through trusts, I no longer do so for three reasons.

First, each trust must have one or more trustees. In practice the trustee either is a bank or one or more members of the family. Bank trust officers view cottages as problematic assets because they require a lot of attention. Trust beneficiaries fight over the cottage, which thrusts the trust officer into the uncomfortable role of mediator. In addition, while trust officers see the cottage expenses, they do not enjoy the days on the beach and the wind rustling the pines. For all these reasons bank trustees are not thrilled about having a cottage in the portfolio.

Having family members serve as trustee isn't necessarily the solution. Whether there is one trustee or a committee of trustees, a trust-based arrangement is inherently undemocratic. The trustee must decide what is best for the family. Contrast this with a LLC-based cottage plan in which smaller decisions may be made by a management committee (effectively the family trustees) but larger decisions (do we add a wing? give a mortgage? sell the cottage?!) may be made by every owner in proportion to his or her share of the cottage. I believe that allowing each person to vote on these matters has important personal and psychological benefits, and so favor the LLC over the trust for holding the family cottage.

Second, recall the carbon monoxide case. If the trustee was negligent in maintaining the heating system, in addition to losing the cottage to a judgment, the trustee's assets would be subject to levy. Banks are heavily insured and have substantial

STRUCTURE OF A TRUST

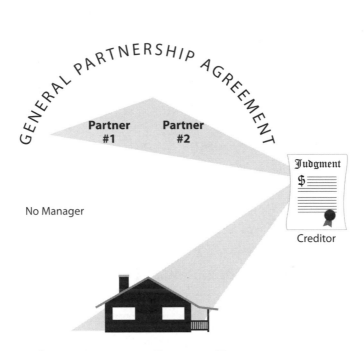

STRUCTURE OF A GENERAL PARTNERSHIP

assets. Family-member trustees, however, could be ruined by our hypothetical lawsuit.

Finally, trusts in most states cannot last more than approximately ninety years. While not all families will succeed in keeping their cottages for (another) ninety years, there is no reason to subject a family whose goal is to keep the family cottage indefinitely to this rule. Limited liability companies are not subject to this rule and so may last indefinitely.

The Limited Partnership

The limited partnership is a hybrid form, sharing characteristics of a general partnership with those of a limited liability entity such as a corporation or limited liability company. The limited partnership is organized by filing papers with state regulators in exchange for which the inactive (limited) partners are granted a shield from creditor claims.

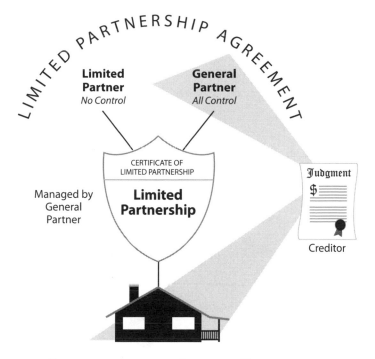

STRUCTURE OF THE LIMITED PARTNERSHIP

A limited partnership, however, by law must have a general partner whose assets are not protected. In a business setting the partner's individual assets are protected by establishing the general partner as a corporation or LLC. While it is possible to implement a cottage plan through a limited partnership, everything that may be accomplished through a limited partnership may be achieved more simply through a close corporation or limited liability company.

The Limited Liability Limited Partnership

A new entity called the limited liability limited partnership is permitted in some states. This form grants the shield of limited liability automatically to all partners and eliminates the need to set up a corporation or LLC to serve as the general partner.

Because the LLLP is not available in all states, and as it affords no advantage over the corporation or LLC for cottage succession planning, I do not consider it further here.

The Corporation

A corporation is an entity established under the laws of a state that, when properly established and maintained, insulates its owners ("shareholders") from personal liability for entity debts. Corporations normally have three tiers of control: shareholders, directors, and officers.

Shareholders exercise ultimate control over the corporation by selecting directors and voting on the most significant corporate

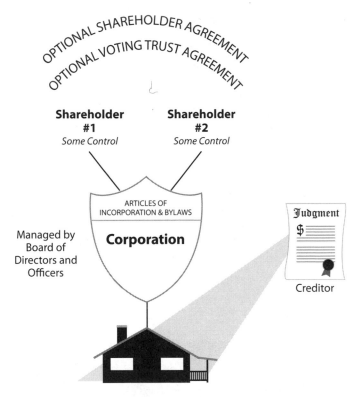

Structure of the Corporation

transactions. The elected directors establish corporate policy and, in turn, appoint officers to carry out the day-to-day business of the corporation.

Some cottages are owned by corporations. An advantage of the corporate form is that it is familiar to many people. Due to the novelty of the LLC, the roles of shareholders, directors, and officers and their interrelationship are better understood than the roles of the "member" and "manager" of a limited liability company. Unlike its owners, a corporation may have perpetual life.

On the other hand, it is difficult to adapt the three-tiered ownership and control structure of a corporation to the family cottage. The family's attorney must draft separate documents — the corporation's articles of incorporation, its bylaws, and other agreements (such as a voting trust, a shareholder agreement, or both) — into a unified system to meet the founder's objectives. This is a difficult task because so many working parts must mesh. If it is hard to draft this system, it also will be hard for the family to work with the resulting documents. Is the prohibition on transfer of an interest in the corporation contained in the voting trust agreement, the shareholder agreement, or the bylaws? Where is the scheduling agreement? Where does it say who has the power to make improvements to the cottage? What if a bylaw provision is inconsistent with the shareholder agreement? Which one controls? Three-tiered ownership may make sense in a business setting, but is unnecessary for the family cottage. Besides, separating control into three levels seems artificial, since the people who own the cottage generally control its use and enjoyment.

An area of grave concern is that the shield of limited liability afforded by a corporation can be lost if the corporation does not observe statutory formalities. Among these formalities, a corporation's shareholders are required to meet annually to elect the board of directors, and an annual report must be filed with the state in which directors and officers are identified. These are the reasons I find the corporation to be less suited to cottage succession planning than the limited liability company.

The Close Corporation

Many states permit a corporation to file an election that eliminates the need for a board of directors and for shareholder meetings. Corporations that file this election are known as **close corporations**. Some have likened close corporations to incorporated partnerships (much like a limited liability company). The relationship of the shareholders to the corporation and its assets may be reduced to a single shareholder agreement.

Close corporations tend to be more expensive to form than regular corporations because an attorney must draft the shareholder agreement, which will be complex if it addresses all matters that it should. A close corporation will be easier to maintain than a regular corporation because annual shareholder and director meetings are not required.

A close corporation that makes the Subchapter S election (described below) would be the best choice for cottage succession planning if the limited liability company were not available. Between the close S corporation and the LLC, I favor the LLC because it is less fragile (no inadvertent termination of S status is possible) and it is more familiar to attorneys and accountants.

The S Corporation

A corporation may elected to be taxed as if it were a partnership. Cottage corporations would do this in order to permit each shareholder to claim his or her proportionate share of the real property tax deduction. The election to be taxed as a partnership

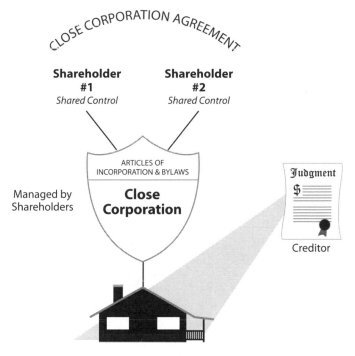

STRUCTURE OF THE CLOSE CORPORATION

— called the "S election" — is made by filing Form 2553 with the Internal Revenue Service.

Subchapter S status is fragile and may be lost inadvertently if a shareholder were to transfer his stock to another corporation or to a trust that does not meet certain requirements. While these issues may be addressed through vigilance and proper agreements, dealing with such complexity can really take the fun out of cottage ownership.

The Limited Liability Company

The limited liability company was designed to combine the key advantage of the corporation (limited liability to its owners) with the multiple advantages of the partnership (simplicity, low cost of

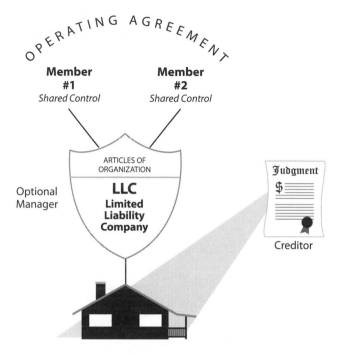

Structure of the Limited Liability Company

formation, flow-through tax treatment, and the latitude it affords attorneys to tailor arrangements suited to specific client requirements). The fact that the LLC is the fastest-growing business form in the country is proof it delivers these promised benefits.

No limited liability company existed before 1977, the year Wyoming first adopted an enabling statute. In 1988 the Internal Revenue Service ruled that the limited liability company would be taxed like a partnership, which generally is viewed by lawyers and accountants as a favorable attribute for a legal entity. This key ruling prompted the remaining states to enact laws to permit the formation of limited liability companies.

Limited liability companies are formed by filing a document ("articles of organization") with the regulators of a state. The state need not be the state in which the cottage is located. In the articles the organizer chooses whether the company will be controlled directly by its owners (a "member-managed" company) or by managers appointed or elected by its owners (a "manager-managed" company).

The articles identify the person to receive notice of any lawsuit involving the company (the "agent for service of process") and the address of the company's office within the state (its "registered office"). Attorneys typically serve as agent for service of process and provide the registered office to their out-of-state clients. The details of a limited liability company-based cottage succession plan remain confidential because the articles of organization provide little information about the company and its property.

Limited liability companies may issue membership certificates to its owners, or may simply use a ledger to keep track of owners and their percentage interest in the company.

Every limited liability company should have an operating agreement. The operating agreement spells out the rights and obligations of each member of the company. My cottage succession planning method uses the limited liability company form of ownership with an operating agreement tailored to the unique requirements of vacation properties. I describe the key features of that operating agreement in Chapters 9 through 14.

Comparing the LLC to the Pretenders

Still skeptical of the value of limited liability companies to your cottage? Let's take a moment to review the key features of the LLC and its competitors.

LLCs and corporations both provide:

+ The ability of the entity to shield cottage owners from the claims of creditors of the entity (limited liability).

SAVING THE FAMILY COTTAGE

- The ability to prevent an owner from filing an action for partition of cottage real estate.

- The ability to pass through taxable income and loss of the members to the entity (this applies only to corporations that have made the "S" election). Both LLCs and corporations are suitable for the cottage that will be rented.

- The ability to hold an endowment (see Chapter 16).

- The ability to amend the governing agreements.

- Favorable treatment under Section 280A of the Internal Revenue Code. This section allows a cottage owner to ignore up to fourteen days of rental income each year. The corresponding cost is that the owner may not depreciate or take expense deductions for a cottage rented for less than fifteen days each year.

- Perpetual existence (the entity never "dies").

For cottage succession planning, a LLC is better than a corporation because:

- The state filing fee usually is less for a LLC.

- The LLC enabling law grants the drafting attorney greater flexibility to meet specific client requirements. This is very important because cottage succession plans must be tailored to each family: there definitely is no one-size-fits-all cottage plan!

- The LLC facilitates keeping ownership in the family line because it is somewhat easier to impose transfer restrictions through a LLC's operating agreement than through corporate documents.

- The LLC fits better with the family culture (LLCs are less formal than regular corporations).

- The LLC is simpler to organize than a corporation.

- The LLC is simpler to maintain (exception: the close corporation is as easy to maintain as a LLC).

- The LLC easily incorporates democratic management principles and is especially well-suited to non-owner control, or to shifting control among owners.

- Collecting assessments from owners and sanctioning a non-paying LLC owner is easier.

- The LLC provides a more favorable tax consequence to its members should they elect to terminate the company and restore to themselves direct real estate law ownership of the cottage.

The Big Picture

In the table on the following page *I compare all of the candidates for cottage planning and conclude that the limited liability company is the best choice.* Answers to the alphabetized questions are rated and totaled.

Comparing Cottage
Ownership Arrangements

Key:

A Can prevent partition lawsuit
B Has perpetual existence
C Filing fees
D Simple to maintain
E Keeps interest in founder's line
F Easy to modify
G Creditor protection
H Take advantage of 14-day rule

I Incorporate democratic principles
J Suited to rental arrangements
K Easy dispute resolution
L Good choice to hold endowment
M Fits with family culture
N Easy to sanction an heir
O Easy to assess an heir
P Easy to set up use schedule

	A	B	C	D	E	F	G	H	I	J	K	L	M	N	O	P	Total
No plan	1	1	4	4	1	4	1	3	1	1	1	1	2	1	1	1	**28**
Ownership Agmt	3	1	4	2	2	2	1	3	3	2	2	1	2	2	2	2	**34**
Irrevocable Trust	4	1	4	3	3	1	2	4	1	2	1	3	2	1	1	1	**34**
General Partnership	3	1	4	2	2	2	1	4	3	3	2	1	2	2	3	2	**37**
Corporation	4	4	1	1	2	2	4	1	2	2	2	2	1	2	2	2	**34**
Limited Partnership	4	1	1	2	2	2	3	4	2	3	2	2	1	2	3	3	**38**
S Corporation	4	4	1	1	2	2	4	4	2	4	2	2	2	2	2	2	**40**
Close Corporation	4	4	1	3	3	3	4	1	4	2	3	2	3	3	3	3	**45**
Close S Corporation	4	4	1	3	3	3	4	4	3	4	3	2	3	3	3	3	**50**
Foreign LLC	4	4	2	2	4	3	4	4	4	4	3	3	4	3	4	3	**55**
Domestic LLC	4	4	3	3	4	3	4	4	4	4	3	3	4	3	4	3	**57**

Scale: A score of 4 means means the entity best achieves the letter objective. For example, a corporation provides creditor protection, so it get a "4" under Column G. An ownership agreement provides no creditor protection, so it gets a "1" under Column G.

Arrangements above the heavy black line do not provide the shield of limited liability; those below the heavy black line provide this shield.

Chapter 9

Welcome to the Club

Like a private club, the members of a limited liability company decide who may become a member. And in your operating agreement you get to lay out the rules of membership.

Language in your operating agreement can keep the cottage in your line of descent — barring the exercise of a member's decision-making power by ex-spouses and creditors — while retaining sufficient flexibility to permit stepchildren to participate in the cottage governance, if that's what the family wants.

In addition, by adopting a "branch" system approach you'll simplify administration, scheduling, and collection of member assessment — while preserving the balance of power among heirs through generations.

Who Is in the Cottage Club?

Deciding who is in the cottage club is done through the company's operating agreement. *If a person is not eligible for membership* *under the operating agreement that person may not be a member of the company even if he or she purchases an interest in the company, receives it as a gift, or acquires the membership interest through legal action.* This simple rule is the key to keeping the company in the founder's line of descent.

For example, if an operating agreement were being drafted for the Keene family it might state:

> No person who is not a descendant of Howard and Helen Keene may become a Member of this company.

A common variation would be:

> No person who is not a descendant of Howard and Helen Keene may become a Member of this company *without the unanimous consent of the members.*

These powerful sentences are adjusted to the specific requirements of each cottage family. A useful refinement is for the operating agreement to describe three categories: automatically permitted transfers, conditionally permitted transfers, and prohibited transfers.

Automatically permitted transfers: The operating agreement should define clearly the types of transfers that may be made without permission from the other members. For instance, cottage LLC operating agreements normally permit an owner to transfer his interest in the company to his descendants or to his estate planning trust without the need for anyone's permission.

The right to pass on a share of ownership in the cottage to a descendant — and the right to govern the cottage that may be attached to that share — goes to the very essence of cottage succession planning. While other family members (especially those without their own children) might like the ability to veto the transfer of membership to an unruly niece or nephew, few families go so far as to reserve this power to the membership. It has something to do with blood being thicker than water. The automatically-permitted transfer clause permits gifts to a descendant of some or all of a member's interest in the cottage LLC during the member's lifetime or after the member's death (e.g. by virtue of provisions in the member's estate planning documents).

Transfers to revocable living trusts are almost always permitted automatically. Many people establish revocable living trusts for estate planning purposes. These trusts can minimize federal estate tax and help avoid the need for probate administration. Little point would be served by requiring the rest of the family to vote on a transfer of a cottage LLC interest to a member's revocable living trust as long as the beneficiary of the trust is the owner or one of his descendants. Some cottage operating agreements require a member who wishes to transfer his interest in the company to an estate planning trust to provide excerpts from the trust to the company. The purpose of this requirement is to allow the family to verify the trust is not being used to transfer an interest in the cottage LLC to an unpermitted person (such as the transferring member's spouse).

Revocable living trusts work well with the cottage LLC. Assume that George, who is forty-two, owns a one-third interest in Sunset Cottage LLC. George has two daughters, Mary and Sarah. Mary is ten and Sarah is twelve. George may use the automatically-permitted transfer provision to assign his membership in Sunset Cottage LLC to his revocable living trust. The trust may provide, for instance, that in case of George's premature death the successor trustee will retain George's membership in Sunset Cottage LLC for the benefit of Mary and Sarah until the younger turns thirty, at which time half of the interest is given to each of them. This arrangement should satisfy everyone: George is comforted by knowing that Mary and Sarah's interest in the cottage will be managed for their benefit until they have attained suitable age and maturity; the family is happy that George's interest stays in the family. The same method can be used to manage the interest of developmentally disabled adults.

While these transfers are automatically *permitted* they are not *required*. Parents do not necessarily have to leave interests to children, particularly those who aren't interested in the cottage.

TRANSFERS PERMITTED ON CONDITION: You may further tailor your operating agreement by allowing transfers with consent of other members or managers.

Stepchildren, adopted children, and same sex-partners can pose delicate problems in cottage succession planning. Some wish to treat stepchildren as blood descendants, others do not. Families often are reluctant to create a blanket rule that treats all stepchildren as automatically permitted transferees for cottage LLC membership shares. What is the solution?

Stepchildren may be classified in the operating agreement as "conditionally permitted transferees." This means a stepchild may become a member only following a vote of company members or managers. You can set the bar high (say, eighty percent of votes) or low (a simple fifty-one percent majority). Either way, such conditional transfers cannot be circumvented. Members may not bypass a vote by giving the stepchild a membership interest in secret or under the member's estate plan. The operating agreement would treat this transfer as void.

PROHIBITED TRANSFERS: Cottage families constantly worry about what will happen to the cottage if one of the cottage owners were to divorce. If you lack a cottage plan, such as a LLC with an operating agreement, you are right to be concerned. Courts may award fractional interests in cottages in divorce settlements to ex-spouses. Those ex-spouses have rights, including the right to force a sale through partition.

Or, the creditor of one owner may take an interest in the cottage and use the threat of partition to force other family members to make good on the debt.

Operating agreements not only can list automatic and conditionally permitted transfers, they also may prohibit certain transfers, treating them as void. This provision is the first line of defense against transfers to a creditor or a member's ex-spouse.

Courts *may* have the power to breach this line of defense, however, so I erect a second line of defense by granting the company or the member who lost his or her interest (to the ex-spouse or creditor) the right to force the ex-spouse or creditor to buy back the interest. The clause in the operating agreement that implements the forced sale may discount the interest and force the seller to accept payment terms. The forced buy-back clause must, however, be reasonable in order to be enforceable against the ex-spouse or creditor.

These provisions help keep ex-spouses and creditors from becoming owners of the family cottage, and for some families, that is reason enough to form a cottage limited liability company.

The Branch Concept

Parents normally distribute their cottages in equal shares to children, and operating agreements often provide that a member's rights and duties are proportionate to their share of the cottage company. If you own a third of the cottage LLC, you get to use the cottage a third of the time and must pay a third of its expenses.

But what happens over time, when, say, Andy's three boys and Carol's two children receive shares, and then Bob, who decided late in life to adopt five children, begins passing on interests to his children? Enter the concept of branches.

A **branch** is one of a number of equal shares of ownership in the cottage LLC. Using this concept in cottage planning reflects the way we're accustomed to thinking about succession: each generation steps into the shoes of its predecessor. The branch concept simplifies scheduling, improves the likelihood of collecting member assessments, and preserves the power structure established when the cottage limited liability company was founded.

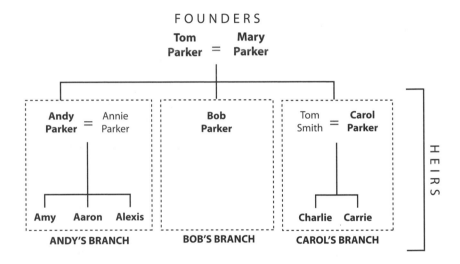

FOUNDERS
Tom Parker = Mary Parker

Andy Parker = Annie Parker — Bob Parker — Tom Smith = Carol Parker

Amy, Aaron, Alexis — Charlie, Carrie

ANDY'S BRANCH — BOB'S BRANCH — CAROL'S BRANCH

HEIRS

SCHEDULING WITHIN A BRANCH SYSTEM: Cottages are seasonal residences. In larger families, competition for slots in the prime season ordinarily can make scheduling difficult. Without the branch concept, Andy, Bob, and Carol would need to juggle the interests and schedules of thirteen owners.

Using the branch concept, Andy, Bob, and Carol each may decide how to split their four weeks of prime season among their own families. The branch concept allows the parent-founder to work things out with his or her children without involving other branches in the decision. This vastly simplifies scheduling of the cottage.

The branch system protects a small branch from encroachment by a larger branch. Without a branch system Carol's two children might be expected to give up some of their time at the cottage to make way for Bob's larger brood. With the branch system Carol's children still may choose to donate some time, but they won't find themselves squeezed out.

Assessments within a branch system: A perennial problem experienced by cottage families is how to handle the owner who does not promptly pay his share of the bills. One approach to nonpayment is to suspend the delinquent member's right to use the cottage until his account is brought current. Taking away a sibling or cousin's right to use the cottage is, however, unpleasant for all concerned. How much better it would be just to collect the money.

The branch system helps avoid the "suspension of use" conflict by providing that the use of *all* branch members is suspended if the assessment of *any* branch member is not paid. Forcing each branch to police its own members relieves the other members of the company (or their branches) from the need to get tough. A wealthier or more responsible member of a branch ordinarily will advance the money necessary to bring the branch's assessments current in order to save his or her vacation.

But what if they don't? What if there is only one member of a branch and he just can't (or won't) pay his share of cottage expenses? The solution is for the operating agreement to grant a **call option** to the company. The call option is a right held by the company to force a defaulting member to sell his membership interest back to the company. In most of the operating agreements I draft, the call option goes into effect if a member is a year or two behind in paying his cottage assessments.

The call option is a counterpart to the **put option** discussed in Chapter 11. The put option is a right *held by the member* to force the company to buy his membership interest in the cottage LLC.

Since the call option and the put option each require the company to pay off a member, these options are written to discourage the exercise of the option. The price the selling member receives is set by a formula. The formula typically discounts the amount the selling member will receive from the company, and the operating agreement requires the selling member to accept installment payments over a number of years. The discounted price and financing terms help the company (e.g. the other cottage owners) find the money to pay off the seller.

Some operating agreements I've drafted impose a deeper discount on the call than on the put. The idea is to discourage a member from defaulting in his obligations to the company. For example, if the put option discounts the price to a selling member by twenty-five percent, the call option might discount that same membership by thirty or thirty-five percent.

One of the things I like about the call is that the remedy is not automatic. The company must choose to exercise it. The company may choose not to exercise its call if the member's failure to pay dues and assessments is for a good reason, such as poor health or financial reversal. The point of the call is to provide a mechanism by which the family can resolve financial disputes without the ugliness of a lawsuit.

BALANCE OF POWER WITHIN A BRANCH SYSTEM: Rare is the family in which wealth remains distributed equally. Cottages, however, tend to operate best when one person does not dominate, but because a privilege of wealth is the ability to buy things, and a cottage is a coveted asset, siblings and cousins holding the short end of the money stick worry that a wealthier cousin sooner or later will acquire their interests in the cottage.

Operating agreements can prevent this from happening and preserve equality among family branches. Some options include designating transfers within the branch as "automatically permitted transfers" and then conditioning the right of a member to transfer his interest outside a branch upon his first offering that interest to members of his own branch. Purchase by the other branch members preserves the equal relationship among the branches.

Another way to preserve equality between branches is to prohibit members from transferring interests to other branches without first offering that interest to the company. This is done by describing a transfer to anyone outside a branch as a "conditionally permitted transfer." The condition to be satisfied is that the interest first must be offered to the company before it may be transferred outside a branch. This rule allows the other branches to pool their funds (by making contributions to the company) to acquire an interest.

Assume a company has four equal branches and a childless member wants to transfer his interest. If the childless member is required to offer his interest to the company and the company completes the purchase, then following the company's purchase three equal branches will remain. The company's purchase preserves branch equality and hence the balance of power. Most families prefer this outcome to permitting one branch to gradually acquire a disproportionately large ownership interest in the cottage LLC.

Operating within a branch system: What if Uncle Charles is getting old and everyone is worried about what he will do with his quarter-share of the family cottage LLC since he had no children or grandchildren. Some nieces and nephews plied him with nice notes and Christmas cards. Will he succumb to their entreaties and skew the balance of ownership between branches of the family?

The operating agreement may be written to address this concern. If you want to retain a balance of ownership and cottage power among branches of families, the operating agreement should treat transfer to the company as an automatically permitted transfer. Since Uncle Charles has no descendants, he essentially is forced to transfer his interest to the company at his death (any other transfer would require company consent, or would violate the operating agreement, thus triggering the discounted buyout clause). The effect of this provision is to preserve the equal ratio among the branches.

It's the year 2025. The ten children of Andy, Bob, and Carol now own all the shares in the cottage limited liability company. One of them, Cathy, Carol's child, wants out. She's childless and is moving to Hong Kong permanently. She owns a sixteen and two-thirds percent interest in the cottage, is entitled to two weeks of prime season there, and would love to sell this all to her favorite cousin, Beth, one of Bob's adopted children, who barely gets enough time at the lake. So what happens?

The answer depends entirely on the operating agreement. Here are some possibilities:

+ Cathy is *permitted* to sell her interest to Beth at any price they can negotiate.

+ Cathy is *not permitted* to sell her interest to Beth *unless* she first offers it to her sister, Clara, at the price offered by Beth.

♦ Cathy is *not permitted* to sell her interest to Beth *unless* she first offers it to Clara at a price Cathy sets. If Clara passes on the purchase, *then* the company has the right to purchase at that price. If the company also takes a pass, Beth may buy.

The first example treats transfers between any descendants of the original owners as permitted transfers. The second example treats it as conditional. The third has multiple conditions and reflects a concern that one heir might gradually acquire control of the cottage by buying up interests as they become available.

Regardless of how your operating agreement is worded, the key is that you get to determine how your cottage will be owned and operated in the future.

Chapter 10

When and How to Organize the Cottage LLC

A limited liability corporation for your cottage can be established right now — a good idea for heirs who already share ownership or parents who want to use a gifting program to reduce estate taxes — or it may be created so it takes effect upon the owners' death.

This chapter describes the step-by-step process you may use to establish your own cottage LLC.

The first decision you will make is whether to create an **Immediate Cottage LLC,** which takes effect, as you'd imagine, immediately, or what I call a **Springing Cottage LLC,** which is designed now, but does not go into effect until its founder's death.

Now: The Immediate Cottage LLC

Immediate Cottage LLCs are a here-and-now transfer from ownership under real estate law to a limited liability company. An Immediate Cottage LLC goes into effect as soon as the cottage owners finalize their operating agreement, file articles of organization, and sign a deed.

Siblings and cousins who own an inherited cottage as tenants in common should develop a cottage LLC and transfer the cottage to it as soon as possible to avoid the problems described in Chapter 5. The same goes for friends or business partners who share vacation property as tenants in common.

As explained in Chapter 15, parents or grandparents who want to make annual exclusion gifts of company membership units must set up an Immediate Cottage LLC. Parents who want to shift the financial or management burden of cottage ownership to their children, or parents who are engaging in Medicaid planning, should establish an Immediate Cottage LLC.

Here are the steps that establish an Immediate Cottage LLC:

1. Choose the state law under which the company will be organized.

2. Confirm that the LLC name the family wants to use is available in that state.

3. Develop the LLC operating agreement (this can take awhile).

4. File articles of organization (some states describe this as a "certificate of formation") with the appropriate office in that state (usually the "Department of Commerce" but sometimes a division of the Secretary of State's office).

5. Transfer the cottage real and personal property to the company by deed and bill of sale or assignment.

6. Have each member sign the operating agreement or an admission agreement (an agreement by which the heir agrees to be bound by the LLC operating agreement).

7. Issue membership certificates to the owners (optional, but a good idea).

8. Confirm property insurance coverage of the cottage and its contents.

9. Maintain the LLC (file income tax returns to claim the property tax deduction and to report any rental income and file any reports required by the state in which the company is organized, holding annual meetings if required by the operating agreement).

Later: The Springing Cottage LLC

A Springing Cottage LLC is set up through an estate plan and takes effect only when the owner dies. Here are the steps that the founder (typically a parent) takes to establish a Springing Cottage LLC:

1. Choose the state law under which the company will be organized.

2. Develop the cottage LLC operating agreement.

3. Amend the parent's revocable living trust and attach the operating agreement as an exhibit to the founder's estate planning document. (Because most cottage owners use a revocable living trust for estate planning, I assume the existence of this type of trust in this chapter. If, however, the estate planning document is a last will and testament, the operating agreement could be appended to the will).

After the founder's death the trustee takes care of steps 2, 4, 5, 7 and 8 as described under Immediate Cottage LLC, and, after the heir signs the operating agreement or an admission agreement (a condition to receiving the gift of the cottage interest), distributes the interest in the LLC to the heir as directed by the founder's trust.

Once the Springing Cottage LLC has been established and ownership has been transferred to the heirs, they operate it just as they would have had their founders established an Immediate Cottage LLC and given the interests to their heirs during the founder's lifetime or under the founder's estate plan.

The Springing Cottage LLC is ideal for founders who want to pass on a family cottage but wish to retain the ability to change their minds about their cottage succession plan. Here's why:

+ A Springing Cottage LLC allows the ancestors to retain full control of the cottage during their lifetimes. This control is especially valuable to those of you who might have to sell the cottage to pay the expense of long-term care, or whose children who have not yet clearly stated whether they want to inherit a share of the cottage.

+ A Springing Cottage LLC does not require you to file an income tax return to claim an income tax deduction for the cottage real property tax, or (in states such as California and Michigan) to risk a property tax increase by virtue of the transfer of the cottage to the company.

+ Refinancing the property is less complicated (lenders are not yet as LLC-friendly as they should be).

+ Homeowner's insurance is simpler to obtain (insurance companies sometimes try to treat the cottage LLC as a business, which increases premiums).

♦ Clients pay no state filing fees or document transfer taxes during their lifetimes.

One of the best things about a Springing Cottage LLC is the ease by which it can be made to take effect. The hardest work of creating a limited liability company — drafting the operating agreement — will have been completed already. The rest can be implemented by the trustee quite easily.

LLC laws may change between the time the operating agreement is drafted and the company is formed. For this reason the trust should permit the trustee to amend the agreement to conform to current law. The trust also may – and in most instances should – permit the operating agreement to be amended with the heirs' unanimous agreement. While it is true the heirs could use this power to avoid the LLC entirely, granting them a power of amendment is reasonable and consistent with the way the operating agreement normally is written.

The Mechanics of LLCs

Once you have decided whether to form an Immediate Cottage LLC or a Springing Cottage LLC, the next steps are:

1. Choosing a state

While it is possible to organize your cottage LLC under the laws of any of our fifty states, my clients usually set the company up under the laws of the state in which they permanently reside (their "home state") or the state in which their cottage is located (the "cottage state").

State LLC laws are similar but not identical. A few states allow the LLC managers to have complete control over the company (most states allow the members to vote on certain major company actions, such as sale of the cottage or dissolution of the company). Some states (most famously, Delaware) draft laws friendly to business interests, thereby hoping to bring work to the state's lawyers, accountants, and bankers. Lawyers can use the greater flexibility afforded by laws of these states to draft documents that maximize protection of the LLC members from creditors.

Assume that Mary and John live in Cincinnati, and have a cottage in northern Michigan. Mary and John's Ohio attorney would be most familiar with the Ohio LLC statute and would prefer to draft an Immediate Cottage LLC operating agreement under Ohio law. If, however, Mary and John opt for a Springing Cottage LLC and none of their children live in Ohio, they might have a Michigan attorney draft an operating agreement under Michigan law.

2. The company name

Two LLCs may not be organized in the same state under the same name. Many families name their company the "Cottage Name LLC" or the "Family Name Cottage LLC." When establishing an Immediate Cottage LLC you may wish to have your attorney reserve the name in the state under which you will organize the company. This step prevents other people from taking that name while you are working on your operating agreement.

Naming the company in advance is not possible when using a Springing Cottage LLC. Names may not be reserved with the state regulators indefinitely, and between the time the operating agreement is drafted and the parents' death, somebody else could organize a company using your preferred name. You may, however, direct the successor trustee of the founder's revocable living trust to include certain words in the name of the company. For instance, if the name of your cottage is "Sunset," you could direct the trustee to include the word "Sunset" in the LLC's name.

3. The operating agreement

This is the key document in cottage succession planning. A cottage LLC operating agreement, which must address the matters discussed throughout this book, is relatively complex. My usual cottage operating agreement is between twenty-five and thirty-five pages long. Some of it is "boilerplate" (the same from document to

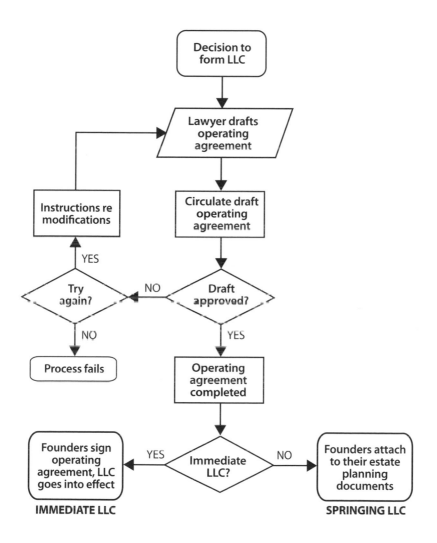

document) while other parts are tailored to the specific (occasionally idiosyncratic) wishes of a client-family.

The process of drafting Springing Cottage LLC operating agreements usually moves quickly and harmoniously. The relative efficiency of the process derives from the fact that the parents can work with their attorney to develop a first draft and then present it to their children for comment. The children usually are very pleased to be receiving the cottage, suspecting that without a structure of some kind they would have problems with their siblings. Children do not wish to appear ungrateful for the gift and usually make constructive suggestions.

The most challenging part of drafting a Springing Cottage LLC usually is establishing a discount rate that both parents (and sometimes their children) consider to be fair (see Chapter 11).

Operating agreements for Immediate Cottage LLCs, on the other hand, especially those owned by cousins, take much longer to complete. An Immediate Cottage LLC cannot be formed without the unanimous agreement of all owners, so cottage plans among siblings and cousins typically go through many revisions before each owner is satisfied. When the property is owned by cousins, some of whom barely know each other, it takes real effort to develop consensus to the point where everyone is willing to sign the operating agreement. Each owner must be persuaded that signing the document improves his or her individual situation.

With siblings and cousins, it is common — and helpful — for one to serve as liaison between the attorney and other owners, collecting comments, distilling concerns and guiding preparation of drafts of the operating agreement. Still, the process can stall, often over miscommunications or misunderstandings (sometimes due to fundamental disagreements). I've found that a conference call often resolves misunderstandings and gets the plan moving again.

The ultimate objective of the drafting process is to develop an operating agreement that captures the wishes of every owner, or at least incorporates the negotiated compromises necessary to achieve a document that each owner is willing to sign. *Once we* *reach this point, however, the fact that the family has aired and worked through concerns contributes to a new spirit of cooperation that bodes well for the future of the cottage.*

4. File the articles of organization with the state office

5. Transfer the cottage property to the LLC

Transferring the cottage to the new LLC is simple — the owners sign a deed naming the LLC as the owner — but there are pitfalls of which you should be aware.

Twenty percent of cottages are mortgaged. If yours is one of them, you should obtain the consent of the mortgage holder to transfer your cottage to the LLC. Failure to take this step could result in a default under the mortgage, allowing the lender to demand immediate repayment. This is potentially costly if the mortgage secures a low, fixed-rate loan. Lenders rarely refuse to consent to a transfer to a cottage LLC, so it is simply prudent to make the request and obtain the lender's written approval prior to deeding the cottage to your LLC.

Cottages that have been in the family for many years often are not protected by title insurance. Cottages that were purchased in the recent past, however, might be insured under a title policy. You should check to see if your cottage is covered by title insurance, and if it is, purchase an endorsement from the insurance company that names the cottage LLC as an additional insured. The endorsement will allow the cottage LLC to make a claim against the insurance company should someone challenge title to your cottage. A more expensive approach — but one that grants the best protection — is to purchase a new title insurance policy in which the cottage LLC is the named insured. If you go this route, you may wish to ask the title company to add to the policy a "non-imputation endorsement." This endorsement precludes the title company from denying coverage following a change of ownership in the company.

I have seen plenty of messy disputes over ownership of cottage contents that could have been avoided had the person who transferred the cottage (usually a trustee or personal representative) remembered that cottages are more than just real estate. They contain furniture, artwork, artifacts, family mementos, docks, lawn mowers, and so on. The deed that transfers the cottage land has no effect upon the cottage contents, so remember that when setting up a cottage LLC, you must transfer the cottage personal property to the company by using a separate document called a "bill of sale" or assignment.

The cottage package may also include boats and even cars (usually old ones). You should discuss with your attorney whether it is advisable to transfer the boats and cars to the company. If you elect to do so, re-register the cars and boats in the company name through the Secretary of State's office and make sure they are properly insured.

6. Members sign the operating agreement and sometimes an admission agreement

An operating agreement is a contract among the members of the company. It defines and governs the relationship of the members to one another and to the company's property, the cottage and its contents. It is fair to call the operating agreement the Cottage Constitution.

To be valid, the agreement must be in writing, and should be signed by the members (while some states do not require signature, I favor requiring each member to sign the document — it makes it harder for them to claim ignorance of what may have become an inconvenient provision in the agreement).

7. Issue membership certificates to owners

Limited liability companies are not required to issue certificates of ownership to their members, but may do so. I like the idea of issuing a membership certificate because it serves as tangible evidence of one's ownership of a share of the company (and indirectly, ownership of the cottage). Membership certificates are one-page forms that identify the owner and indicate how many units in the company are held by that owner. Certificates facilitate transfers of interest in the company. The alternative is to keep track of unit ownership in a ledger or spreadsheet.

There is no set number of membership units. You may have three or three million. I like to have a lot of units so that, as the company's ownership passes down the generations and the number of owners grows (recall The Rabbit Problem described on page 22), it is less likely that fractional units will be required.

8. Confirm insurance coverage

When forming a LLC you also should pay careful attention to your homeowner's insurance. Some insurance companies do not yet understand the role of limited liability companies in family succession planning and attempt to charge a commercial rate on the company's property. These companies assume that the LLC is engaged in some form of business rather than the LLC's true role as a convenient vehicle for holding a family cottage. Check with your insurance agent before transferring the cottage to the new LLC. If the agent insists the commercial rate applies, ask if you can instead maintain conventional homeowner's insurance and name the company as an additional insured.

You also should confirm that the insurance policy covers the cottage contents and, if you have transferred boats or cars to the company, that these assets are insured properly.

The Role of the Attorney

Although it is simple to organize a limited liability company — just fill out a few pages on a form and send it with filing fee to a state office — it is not simple to prepare the company's operating agreement. This demands a thorough understanding of how LLCs are structured, how they operate, and the constraints imposed by the laws of the state in which the company is established. The sample table of contents to a cottage operating agreement found in the appendix illustrates the complexity of this document.

Cottage operating agreements are especially challenging to draft. Although most business attorneys have a generic LLC operating agreement, adapting this to the special requirements of cottage succession planning takes time and thought. If you're launching a cottage succession plan, I recommend screening attorney candidates with the following questions:

- Do you agree that a LLC is the right vehicle to use for our cottage succession plan? If not, what solution do you recommend, and why?

- If you agree that a LLC should be used, how will you draft the operating agreement to address these issues (you may expand this list, of course):
  - Keeping ownership in my line of descent.
  - Allocating control of the company among branches and different generations of owners.
  - Balancing the interests of poorer and richer owners.

+ Scheduling use of the cottage.

+ Handling a member who refuses to pay his share of company expense.

If you're comfortable with the answers, ask the attorney for a written fee agreement that describes what he or she will do and how the fee will be computed. While it is difficult to place a value on a plan that keeps the cottage in your family for generations, the legal fee for a LLC-based cottage plan probably will range from $2,000 to $5,000. Fees typically are in the lower end of this range for a Springing Cottage LLC and the higher end of the range for an Immediate Cottage LLC involving siblings or cousins who have difficulty achieving consensus. The fee range assumes only work on a cottage succession plan, and not related tax planning, estate planning, or real estate consultation. The cost for these legal services should be measured against the expense of a partition case, the family anguish averted, and the value of keeping the cottage in a family for generations.

Some families have their cottage LLC operating agreement drafted by an attorney who specializes in cottage law. That attorney's work should be reviewed by the family attorney to ensure that the cottage LLC fits properly with the family's estate plan, and that the proposed articles of organization and operating agreement conform to the laws of the state in which the company will be established.

The attorney who prepares your cottage succession plan is governed by a strict code of ethics. Among other things, the code requires the attorney to act competently, to avoid conflicts of interest, and to protect a client's confidential information. If the cottage succession plan is created for parents who intend to pass the cottage to their children, the parents are the clients. Estate planning attorneys are familiar with engagements of this nature and are sensitive to the potential conflict of interest that can arise if two parents do not agree upon how the cottage plan should be written.

Creating a cottage succession plan for siblings and cousins places an attorney into a potential conflict of interest. An attorney owes his client the duty of confidentiality and loyalty. Communications between the attorney and his client are subject to an attorney-client privilege, which means the attorney may not disclose confidential communications to anyone else without the client's consent.

A reasonable question is whether an attorney may assist more than one family member when a cottage plan is being developed. The answer is that the attorney may do so if there is no active dispute among the family over the cottage, the attorney explains to each member of the family that the attorney has a possible conflict of interest, the family agrees the attorney may act for more than one member in developing a cottage plan, the family understands that nothing said to the attorney must be kept secret from other members of the family, and realizes that the attorney will withdraw from the matter if a family member insists the attorney hold material information in confidence. Each family member who participates in the development of the plan should acknowledge these things in writing.

I have not found the application of these rules to be an obstacle in my cottage planning practice. To the contrary, siblings and cousins appreciate my role as an "honest broker" whose mission is to bring the family to consensus for their mutual benefit.

Chapter 11

THE COTTAGE
SAFETY VALVE

A prime reason for creating a cottage limited liability company is to prevent any co-owner from forcing a sale by filing a partition lawsuit. The company helps keep the cottage in the family for generations.

But what about family members who don't want to be there? Trapping someone in cottage ownership surely will lead to unhappiness all around. The trapped member will make everyone miserable — the antithesis of a cottage plan.

So what's the answer? A good cottage plan will allow family members to make graceful exits on terms that permit the rest of the family to be able to afford to keep the cottage. The flexibility of the LLC allows you to craft this compromise: give the heir the right to sell his interest back to the company, but at a reduced price and with favorable financing for the company. The heir's right to compel the company to purchase the heir's membership interest is called a **put option** or "put."

When drafting cottage plans I spend a lot of time discussing the put with my clients. In many ways it is the 21st century's equivalent to the right of partition. We must establish the put price, the financing terms imposed on the selling member, and when that member may exercise the put.

The Put Price

The price an exiting member is to receive (the "put price") is set by a formula in the operating agreement. The first part of the formula is:

Basic Put Price Formula

Put Price = MOS x VC

Where MOS is the Member's Ownership Share and VC is the Value of the Company.

If, for example, the exiting member owned one-quarter of the units of the family limited liability company, his MOS would be twenty-five percent. Some operating agreements refer to this fraction as the member's "sharing ratio."

Three Methods for Valuing the Company

Three main methods are used to establish the value of the company: a stipulated value, a value derived from the property tax assessment, and a value based upon appraisal.

Some families fix the company value in the operating agreement. The fixed value might be the worth of the cottage at the time it was inherited or a negotiated figure. While this method has the appeal of simplicity, if the property has appreciated in the years after the value is fixed the exiting heir will receive considerably less than the fair value of his share of the cottage. The ability to exercise an "in the money" put also might lead to a stampede for the door. Conversely, in a falling market (which, believe it or not, can happen) the purchasing heirs will be asked to pay more than the membership interest is worth (good luck). The stipulated value formula might provide:

SETTING THE VC — STIPULATED VALUE

$$VC = \mathbf{\$600,000} + CC + CPP - CD$$

Where VC is the Value of the Company, CC is the amount of company cash, CPP is the value of the company's personal property and CD is the amount of company debt.

The stipulated price method may be simple, but introduces substantial risk into the equation. I do not favor this method.

In states that have a property tax the assessor is required to value the property each year. Cottage owners can take advantage of this "free" appraisal and incorporate government assessments into put formulas. For instance, an operating agreement might provide:

SETTING THE VC — ASSESSED VALUE

$$VC - \textbf{\textit{assessed value}} + CC + CPP - CD$$

Incorporating the assessor's valuation into the computation allows the put price to be determined by looking at the most recent tax bill. This method avoids a "battle of appraisals" in which the selling family member hires an appraiser (hoping for a high value) and the buyer (whether another family member or the company itself) hires a second appraiser and seeks a low value.

The disadvantage of this method is that the assessor's opinion of the cottage's value will seem too low to likely sellers and too high to likely buyers. The lack of faith in the assessor's opinion leads some of my clients — particularly those with a business or real estate background — to insist the cottage be valued by a professional appraiser.

In this instance the operating agreement would provide:

Setting the VC — Appraised Value

VC = **appraised *value*** + CC + CPP – CD

Business agreements often use the appraisal method. Some agreements require the parties to select a single appraiser and stipulate they will use the value set by that appraiser. Other agreements start there, but allow a party who disagrees with the first appraiser's value to hire, at that party's expense, a second appraiser. The put formula uses the average of the two appraisals. Still other agreements require each party to hire his own appraiser and for the designated appraisers to select a *third* (presumably neutral) appraiser, whose value then is used in the formula.

There are many variations, but the gist is that the more appraisals there are the more accurate the price is and the more expensive the process is. The agreements that rely upon one appraisal ordinarily impose the appraiser's fee on the company. Those that use two appraisals require the exiting heir to pay for one appraisal and for the company to pay for the other appraisal. The agreements that rely upon three normally split the appraisal costs equally between the selling heir and the company.

States regulate appraisers through a licensing process. Appraisers with limited experience hold one form of license and experienced appraisers receive another. Operating agreements that rely upon appraisal often specify minimum qualifications for the appraisers who will value the cottage. A common requirement is that the appraiser be a "MAI," meaning that he or she is a Member of the Appraisal Institute (an organization that admits only appraisers who meet the Institute's experience and education criteria).

The Discount

Most of the cottage succession plans that I draft impose a discount on the price paid for the interest of the exiting heir. The discount, of course, comes straight from the pocket of the exiting heir.

Assume that Andy, Bob, and Carol each own one-third interests in a cottage LLC, and that the cottage owned by the company is appraised to be worth $600,000. Bob decides to move permanently to Berlin. His one-third interest in the LLC nominally is worth $200,000. When Andy, Bob, and Carol set up the company, however, they agreed that should a member decide to sell out the company would have the obligation to buy the seller's membership interest at seventy percent of its appraised value. The operating agreement further provides that the company need pay only twenty percent of the purchase price as a down payment and would give the selling member a promissory note for the balance, payable over ten years. The note would bear interest at the prime rate, fixed as of the date of the note.

Andy reminds Bob of the clause in the operating agreement. Bob no longer is quite so sure he wants to sell, since he'd receive only $140,000 — $28,000 at closing, and a promissory note for $112,000 for the balance. The upshot: if Bob does decide to cash out, Andy and Carol are far more likely to be able to afford to keep the cottage than if they had to pay Bob $200,000 in cash.

Discounting the price that will be received by the heir who exercises his put has three effects: 1) it emphasizes that the family's interest in preserving the cottage is more important than the economic benefit the cottage confers upon a single heir; 2) it discourages an heir from selling (the heir doesn't get full value for the interest); and 3) it compensates the rest of the family for the burden of finding the money to pay off the former owner through the advantageous price at which the company buys the interest.

Founders impose a small discount if they view the cottage more as a financial asset in which the heir's inheritances are invested temporarily.

Founders impose a steep discount on the transferred membership if they view the cottage as a place of recreation and not primarily as a financial asset. A steep discount and extended time for payment at a company-friendly interest rate helps avoid the need to sell the cottage or put a big mortgage on it. The cottage stays in the family because the "non-exiting" heirs can afford to buy out the "exiting" heir. Families that favor steep discounts usually have these characteristics:

+ They've owned the cottage for a long time.

+ The family is large.

+ The family is emotionally attached to the cottage.

+ The family places a high value on preserving the cottage for future generations.

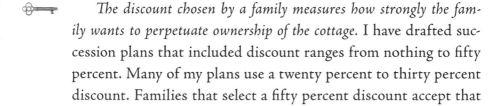

The discount chosen by a family measures how strongly the family wants to perpetuate ownership of the cottage. I have drafted succession plans that included discount ranges from nothing to fifty percent. Many of my plans use a twenty percent to thirty percent discount. Families that select a fifty percent discount accept that an exiting heir will not receive the economic value of that heir's interest in the cottage. They value keeping the cottage in the family more highly than preserving that heir's inheritance.

Conversely, families that use a zero discount or even ten percent are, in effect, giving each heir the opportunity to convert the investment from cottage form to cash. Parents with less affluent children tend to use a lower discount.

Discounting the put price places the family's interest in keeping the *cottage ahead of the individual's interest. This principle distinguishes family-centric cottage planning from individual-centric common law.*

The Put Terms

The operating agreement ordinarily requires the exiting heir to accept the sale price in installments and not as a lump sum. The operating agreement also states the proportion of the price that is paid at closing, the number of years over which the balance is to be paid, the rate at which interest is charged on the unpaid balance, and the collateral that the exiting heir will receive. By incorporating financing terms into the operating agreement, the remaining heirs avoid the closing costs, fees, and complications of a bank loan.

Financing terms also can benefit the exiting heir. If the exiting heir's inability to afford to remain in the cottage is due to improvidence, then providing to that heir a modest down payment (perhaps ten percent to twenty percent of the purchase price) and a stream of payments over a period of years is in the nature of a family annuity.

Not all families have the money to simply write a lump-sum check to the exiting heir. The operating agreements I draft give the company the right to pay for the exiting heir's share over a period of years, typically five to fifteen, with a down payment of ten percent to twenty-five percent. The operating agreement allows prepayment of the loan. This enables the company to pay off the exiting heir at any time. This provision is handy if relations between the exiting heir and the rest of the family are strained. The company may borrow the payoff funds from other members or from a bank. Normally, however, the company prefers to avoid bank financing with its associated appraisal fees, title search fees, and other costs.

The company will owe a large sum to the exiting heir after making the required down payment. The Internal Revenue Code requires the company to pay a minimum rate of interest on the amount due. The Internal Revenue Service publishes this minimum rate, called the "applicable federal rate," monthly. While some families adopt the AFR, I prefer to use the National Mortgage Contract Interest Rate because it approximates the average mortgage interest rate. Of course the founders may choose any interest rate it deems fair, such as the prime rate. The interest rate may be fixed as of the date of the purchase or may be adjusted at intervals — I recommend annual adjustments to simplify the interest rate computation — as specified in the operating agreement.

The company should give collateral to the heir to protect the heir from the company's failure to pay the heir on time. A recent study found that over eighty percent of cottages are owned free and clear, so the company has a terrific source of collateral: the cottage. The exiting heir will receive a security interest in the form of a mortgage or deed of trust, which the exiting heir must discharge after having been repaid in full.

While an alternative to granting the exiting heir a lien on the cottage would be to give the heir a security interest in the remaining owners' shares in the company (a pledge), this rarely is satisfactory to the exiting heir.

When a put may be exercised: The operating agreement should limit members' ability to exercise their puts. For instance, what would happen if members owning half of the company suddenly exercised their puts? The company would be hard-pressed to honor the puts despite being obligated to do so.

One approach would be to cap the indebtedness of the company at an amount established by the founders — perhaps $100,000 or $250,000. This amount represents the level of debt the company's members could reasonably be expected to repay. Another approach would be to provide in the operating agreement that no member may exercise a put if a previously exercised put remains unpaid. If more than one member decides to exercise his put at the same time the exercise privilege may be allocated by flipping a coin.

The put is the cottage succession plan's safety valve. It allows an heir to make a relatively graceful exit from the cottage (especially when compared to a partition lawsuit). The put formula allows each family to strike its unique balance between the financial interests of an individual heir and the interests of all other heirs in keeping the cottage in the family.

Chapter 12

COTTAGE DEMOCRACY

One of the beauties of the cottage limited liability company is that it can be structured to incorporate democratic principles. The people get to vote (or their representative does) on everything from buying a new dishwasher to painting the shutters robin's-egg blue. Should we rebuild the porch? *Let's vote.* Should we buy a new boat? *The nays have it.* Democracy is at play in these decisions regardless of whether the cottage is owned by a *member*-managed or *manager* managed company.

A family must choose between these methods for controlling the LLC. A *member*-managed LLC is a direct democracy. This works well when cottage companies are owned equally by a small number of people, such as siblings. A *manager*-managed LLC, on the other hand, is a representative democracy. This form is ideal for cottage companies with many owners.

Let's look at some of the ways in which these management forms can play out.

Member Management

Our three siblings, Andy, Bob, and Carol, want to keep things simple and select member-management. Each, however, is worried about being outvoted by the other two on some issue of importance or another.

Andy uses the cottage frequently. He is worried Bob and Carol will vote to rent out the cottage during the summer, thus interfering with his sacred retreat. Carol, who lives near the cottage, has access to the lake and likes the idea of some extra income to defray cottage expenses. Bob often is posted overseas for years at a time and also would like to be able to rent the cottage, at least during "his" weeks. Simple majority rule, which would work for most things, doesn't satisfy Andy, who wants the ability to veto rental of the cottage. Provided Bob and Carol agree, we can put cottage rental into a special category that requires the unanimous agreement of the members.

Bob, meanwhile, is more affluent than Andy or Carol, and worries his siblings might want to mortgage the cottage to raise money. Bob doesn't like the idea of cottage-as-ATM-machine, and wants to be able to approve (or veto) any mortgage that his siblings might propose.

Andy and Bob agree to each other's restrictions. Carol agrees, and we enshrine their deal in the final operating agreement.

At some point in my explanation of cottage management one of my clients usually asks, "Why don't we just require every decision to be unanimous?" I do not favor requiring unanimity because it subverts the basic principle of the cottage democracy — subordination of the wishes of one to the will of the majority. The ability to veto every proposal places too much power in the hands of an unreasonable person. This is why the list of decisions to be made by unanimous agreement should be kept short.

Using Managers

The member-managed LLC becomes unwieldy if there are more than three owners (four risks deadlock and five is a lot of people to convene for routine decision-making). The solution is for the operating agreement to permit members to designate one or more company "managers."

The manager may have only a little power or tremendous power — it is up to the members. A few states (such as Delaware) allow managers to have total power over the company. This flexibility in allocating power (control) over the company is one of the chief advantages of the limited liability company form.

For example, I met with the five Marsh children to discuss forming a LLC for the Lake Michigan cottage they'd inherited. Before the meeting one of the children told me some of her siblings didn't always get along. She added that two of the five were fairly well off but the other three struggled to get by. Despite these differences, each of the children wanted to find a way to share the cottage and pass their shares on to their children. How might they do this?

We agreed that member-management would be awkward if five of them had to be consulted for each decision, and that things would only get worse as they passed interests on to their own children. I said that manager-management was the way to go.

I explained it was up to them how to structure the management, but they might consider either a three-person or five-person management committee to handle most of the company's operations. Since there were five branches (one for each child and his or her descendants), a management committee comprised of a representative from each branch could have great power. The disadvantage of this approach was that it was not much more efficient than member-management.

I suggested they instead consider a three-person management committee. Because all branches would not be represented on the committee, I proposed the committee have relatively little authority. Basically, I said, the committee would oversee the usual operation of the cottage, but would not be able to decide anything on the "reserved list." This list, which would identify matters in which each member would want a say, might contain these items:

- Adopt annual cottage budget.

- Amend the Articles of Organization of the company.

- Amend the operating agreement.

- Approve capital improvements.

- Approve actions that would change the character of the cottage.

- Assess the members for more than their share of the property taxes, property insurance, and regular maintenance expense.

- Convert company to different legal form.

- Dissolve the company.

- Establish a cottage use fee.

- Merge the company.

- Mortgage the cottage.

- Permit rental of the cottage.

+ Require contribution to endowment.

+ Select or replace any manager.

+ Sell the company or the cottage.

We worked through this list and adjusted the authority of the management committee until all five owners were satisfied the management committee would not have too much power, but that it would have sufficient power to operate the cottage efficiently.

Next we discussed an allocation of duties within the management committee. Each cottage, I've found, requires somebody to write checks, somebody to make sure the maintenance is done, and, in larger families, somebody to schedule use of the cottage.

Allocating each of these functions to different members of the management committee works well. Fewer things slip through the cracks if responsibility for a function is assigned to one person. If each of these managers is on the committee, they can call upon one another when items cross categories. For instance, the person in charge of maintenance might need a check, or wonder if there is money in the budget for a certain repair, and can take the matter up with the person in charge of finances either directly or at the next meeting of the management committee.

The Marsh heirs had me allocate cottage operation responsibilities into their operating agreement this way:

MAINTENANCE AND OPERATIONS MANAGER: Under the direction of the Management Committee, the Maintenance and Operations Manager shall maintain and improve the cottage, its utility systems (water, septic, telephone, etc.), fixtures, and associated personal property. The Maintenance and Operations Manager shall deliver a proposed maintenance budget to the Financial Manager by October 31 each year.

FINANCIAL MANAGER: Under the direction of the Management Committee, the Financial Manager shall carry out the financial directives of the Management Committee, including billing and collecting regular assessments from each member and such other sums from each member as determined by the Management Committee; maintaining bank accounts; preparing and filing returns and forms with units of federal, state, or local government as are required; and preparing and distributing periodic accountings to the Management Committee and to each member, in a form and at such times as directed by the Management Committee, provided, however, that such accountings shall always be made available to the Management Committee at least ten days in advance of its quarterly meetings.

The Financial Manager shall prepare the first draft of the annual budget, and present it to the Management Committee before December 1 each year. The budget shall establish expenditure categories and the maximum amount that may be spent during the following calendar year within each category. The company budget shall be adopted by the Management Committee by December 31 after making such revisions as the Management Committee deems advisable.

SCHEDULING AND RECORD-KEEPING MANAGER: Under the direction of the Management Committee, the Scheduling and Record-Keeping Manager shall schedule use of the cottage by the members. The Scheduling and Record-Keeping Manager shall report all use of the cottage to the Financial Manager and the Management Committee.

The Scheduling and Record-Keeping Manager shall be the official custodian of the Company's records and shall respond to Member requests for records as required by law.

Notices required to be given to the Company shall be given to the Scheduling and Record-Keeping Manager, who shall disseminate such notice promptly to the other Managers and members.

The Scheduling and Record-Keeping Manager shall file the annual Company report required by the Limited Liability Company Act each year no later than the deadline (currently February 15), and shall file such other statements and returns with federal, state, and local authorities as required by law.

The Marsh family agreed the management committee would be elected by the members annually, and that the management committee itself would determine who would serve as the Maintenance and Operations Manager, Financial Manager, and the Scheduling and Record-Keeping Manager. The allocation of control between the members and the management committee, and the limitations upon the power of the management committee, assured the family that the oldest child would not be able to dominate the cottage as his siblings feared.

Chapter 13

Scheduling and Use

The payoff for all the work that goes into owning a cottage is the pleasure of actually *using* the cottage. But who gets to use the cottage, and when? This is the terrain of scheduling and use provisions, which are vital to the smooth and satisfying operation of a shared cottage.

Cottage sharing at its best accommodates the varying needs of all involved, creates happy memories, and strengthens bonds among the entire family. Cottage sharing at its worst, however, can be a source of deep conflict, aggravating sibling rivalries, creating spats over dog hair and rowdy nephews, or causing long-lasting family rifts over the handling of cottage use by parents, renters, or the spouses of deceased siblings. And as cottage families expand (The Rabbit Problem again), the logistics of planning cottage time becomes increasingly challenging due to members' busy and sometimes inflexible schedules.

Families avoid these perils by developing a fair system for allocating cottage time, one that reflects the family's values, traditions, and needs. Scheduling systems describe how owners apportion cottage use among themselves and others, such as guests and even renters.

I've observed three primary arrangements commonly used for scheduling cottage use, none of which is ideal. With **Ad Hoc** systems telephone calls and emails are exchanged until a consensus schedule emerges from the fog. With the **Customary Slots** system, cottage use has settled into a predictable same-time-next-year pattern, with the same owners using the cottage the same weeks each year. Finally, with a **Founder Control** approach current owners take their weeks and then fit the rest of the family into the remaining time. Family members say when they prefer to visit and the founders sort it out. Some weeks are more desirable than others (Memorial Day, Independence Day, Labor Day, the annual summer party), so founders may encourage the whole family to convene then or create an informal rotation for in-demand weeks.

When founders cede control or die, heirs to a founder-controlled cottage can be left without a useable system. The Ad Hoc approach depends entirely upon the goodwill of the participants, something that can't be guaranteed over the long haul. Siblings who have grown up sharing things amicably often can work things out. Cousins, who inhabit the more distant suburbs in the family geography, may have a harder time with the Ad Hoc system. The Customary Slots system works well — until somebody has a commitment that conflicts with the slot. Like snowstorms affect airlines, rearranging time slots can create a ripple of disruptive complications for all.

Creating a Fair and Sustainable Cottage Sharing System

Creating a simple system for cottage sharing requires fore-thought and reflection on family traditions and needs. Systems must address two things: 1) how time is divided and 2) who else may use the cottage, including parents, surviving spouses, pets, youthful relatives, renters, and guests.

A sustainable cottage-sharing system has the following attri-butes:

+ It is as simple as possible.

+ It grants use in proportion to ownership shares of the cottage.

+ It is mathematically fair.

+ It respects family traditions and fits the family culture.

+ It accommodates rentals if desired by the family.

+ It permits members to exchange time slots by mutual agreement.

+ It produces a clear schedule.

Time may be divided among owners in two basic ways: a **time-sharing model** or a **rooming-house model** (first-come, first-served).

Some families prefer to allocate time slots during which an owner and the owner's immediate family have exclusive use. This pattern emerges when either the cottage is too small to host large groups or when owners view it as a place of retreat — even from (or maybe *especially* from) family. I call this system, which divides the year into discrete exclusive-use periods, the time-sharing model.

Other families take a "there's always room for one more" approach to using their cottages. The rooming-house model is possible only if the cottage is large enough to accommodate more than one branch of the family at a time. The cottage then serves as the hub around which the spokes of the extended family turn. George Howe Colt's homage to the family cottage, *The Big House*, illustrates the rooming-house model.

It is possible to meld the time-sharing and rooming-house models by allowing members exclusive cottage use for a portion of the season and by establishing dedicated "all are welcome" periods.

Let's examine each approach separately and then look at considerations for additional cottage users.

The Time-Sharing Model

Creating a time-sharing model, which is used by most of my clients, is essentially a math project. It is implemented in three steps: defining the seasons, dividing the seasons, and establishing a process to assign time slots.

First, we define two seasons. **Prime season** is the high-demand period; **off season** is the rest of the year. A maintenance period during which no one may use the cottage may also be established.

It is helpful to define prime season as a fixed number of weeks. Ideally the number of weeks is evenly divisible by the number of branches in the family. For instance, a family with three branches would find it useful to divide prime season into exactly nine or twelve weeks. Agreement language reflecting this may read as follows:

The" prime season" is a period of nine consecutive weeks that includes the entire months of July and August. The remainder of the year is the "off season."

or

The "prime season" begins exactly twelve weeks before the Saturday before Labor Day each year. The "off season" shall be the remainder of the year.

or

"Prime season" is designated as a period beginning on the Friday before Memorial Day and ending on the Tuesday after Labor Day. The remainder of the year is the "off season."

The next step is to divide prime season into equal segments. The length and number of time slots depends on family custom and convenience. Families with two equal branches, for instance, might divide the prime season in half and swap halves annually. Or, they might divide prime season into one- to three-week segments and then allocate time by stipulation, agreement, or lottery.

Following this pattern families with three equal branches would divide a twelve-week prime season into segments of one, two, or four weeks; families with four branches would divide prime season into segments of one, two, or three weeks; and those with six branches would divide it into one- or two-week segments. This system works best by matching time-segment length to the longest vacation ordinarily taken by the families involved.

Cottage owners should adjust the definition of prime season to fit its use patterns. A twelve-week prime season, however, is very common because it permits equal division of the summer among two, three, four, or six branches.

The final step in the time-sharing model is to allocate time segments equitably. This is not as difficult as it might seem. A simple approach is to create a priority system. Some families cut cards, others draw straws, still others award priority by age or by geographic distance from the cottage. The branch with the highest priority has the first pick of time slots, the second branch gets second pick, and so on, until the calendar is filled. Once this is done families may swap times by mutual consent. The following year the selection order rotates: the second family picks first, the third family picks second, and so on. Over the years each family branch will have held first, last, and all intermediate priority positions. The selection priority is established in the system's first year. This system avoids the need for an annual lottery. People know in advance the priority they'll have. The system is mathematically fair. And it is flexible — weeks may still be swapped (or shared) by mutual agreement.

Off season is much easier to schedule. While it is possible to allocate use in the same way as the prime season, it is more common to allow branches to use the cottage on a first-come, first-served basis. Larger families ordinarily designate a scheduling manager, someone who keeps track of requests for off-season use and helps reconcile conflicts. Some families designate the holidays as a shared-use period during which all are welcome up to the capacity of the cottage.

The Rooming-House Model

A small number of the plans I prepare use the rooming-house model. In its pure form this model — which is more common within families that own several cottages or one very large cottage — allows owners to use the cottage to its capacity throughout the year. One variation of the rooming-house model establishes priorities *among* branches of the family and *within* branches of the family.

Each individual owner tells the scheduling manager when they'll be using the cottage. The scheduling manager checks the master schedule and the owner may use the cottage as long as there is room at the inn. If too many owners have requested the cottage for a particular period, the scheduling manager allocates use based upon the branch and owner priorities. The branch priorities typically change from year to year (using a rotation such as the one described above in the time-share section). Within branches, however, the older generation normally retains the higher priority, with a rotation among the younger generation in the interest of fairness.

Mix It Up: The Blended Model

A third alternative to allocating time is a blended model, which attempts to combine the best features of the time-sharing and rooming-house models. The big holidays, and possibly some additional weeks, are set aside so the extended family is welcomed at the cottage up to its capacity. The balance of the prime and off seasons are allocated on the time-sharing model. The blended model seeks to balance the feelings of those who cannot get enough of family and those who can.

Cottage Users

All cottage-scheduling systems proceed from the premise that use rights are proportionate to ownership. This is logical: if you are paying a quarter of cottage expenses, it is reasonable to expect you'll enjoy the cottage one-quarter of the time. This simple rule is subject to modification by agreement. For instance, many cottage operating agreements suspend cottage-use rights if a member fails to pay his "dues." The deadbeat's time is made available to owners whose dues are current. The rationale for this rule is that one should not enjoy the benefits of cottage ownership if one has not met its burdens.

If permitted in the cottage LLC operating agreement, owners also may make the cottage available to non-members such as parents, spouses of deceased siblings, children, family friends, guests, and renters. Use by these non-owners can be a happy or unhappy experience. It is wise to individually address each of these visitor categories in the course of developing a cottage-sharing plan.

Parents

Children who receive cottages as gifts from parents ordinarily allow Mom and Dad to use the cottage at any time. Parents who do not want the value of their cottage to be included in their estates, however, may have to pay fair market rent to their children for this use (see Chapter 15).

Children who purchase their cottages from parents may not view the matter as generously. A cottage large enough to accommodate parents and children may pose few problems. If the cottage is not large, however, and children wish to allow the parent to continue to use the cottage following the purchase, an agreement among the children to yield their time proportionately is a good idea. For example, one family I worked with purchased the cottage from their mother. The three siblings had me guaranty in the operating agreement the mother's equal use rights. As a result the prime season was divided into four equal parts even though the cottage was owned by the three children.

Surviving Spouses

Keeping cottage ownership within the family is a pillar of cottage succession planning, so cottage plans typically bar owners from transferring a share to a surviving spouse (whether during an owner's lifetime or under the terms of an estate plan).

Families that acknowledge an in-law's affinity for the cottage may grant them some use rights. The most common arrangement I see in my practice is to allow a non-member surviving spouse subordinate use rights in the cottage. In other words, if nobody else is using the cottage, the surviving spouse may use it. Other families don't feel the need to accommodate the surviving spouse and grant no such rights, reasoning that surviving spouses may be guests of their children at the cottage.

Members who have uneasy relationships with other cottage owners (usually siblings) may worry that, if they die, their surviving spouse will not be welcome at the cottage. These owners try to enshrine their surviving spouse's use rights in the operating agreement. Other members usually express concern about this guaranty, worrying what will happen if the surviving spouse remarries and brings a group of strangers into the cottage mix.

By way of compromise between the extremes of barring the non-member surviving spouse from the cottage and giving the spouse the guaranteed right to use the cottage for life, many families state in the operating agreement that the surviving owners will decide whether — and under what circumstances — a non-member surviving spouse will be allowed to use the cottage. This is a good solution because the surviving spouse's rights may be terminated by the other owners should circumstances (or their relationship with the spouse) change. The surviving spouse, meanwhile, knowing his or her right to use the cottage may be terminated at any time, is more likely to strive for a harmonious relationship with owners than would the surviving spouse with guaranteed use rights.

In all cases, the operating agreement must make it clear that the non-member surviving spouse is not an owner, has no rights that may be sold or transferred, and that the surviving spouse's use rights terminate when he or she dies.

Guests and Younger Family Members

Recall Carol and Tom, who live near the cottage and have two boys in college. Summer is Tom's busiest season and the boys have time on their hands so they plan to use the cottage whenever Uncle Andy's family and Uncle Bob won't be up. Boys will be boys and word of some pretty wild parties got back to Carol and Tom. The blue-hairs down the beach were not amused — the splashing and carousing wrecked their canasta party.

The first decision a cottage family must make regarding guests is whether they may use the cottage if an owner is not present. Some families like to use the cottage as a guesthouse, in which case they would permit unescorted guests to use the cottage. These families would, of course, impose rules for the safety of their guests, such as limiting use of boats and other equipment to guests of suitable age and maturity. Many families, however, incorporate into the operating agreement a rule that guests may be at the cottage only if an owner is there. The owner-sponsor is responsible for the enjoyment and safety of the guest and is accountable to the other owners for any damage caused by the guest.

Families often adopt a rule that limits unescorted access to the cottage by college-age or younger adults.

Pets

The late afternoon sun banked off the lake and streamed golden through the window, illuminating the wisps of dog hair floating through the room. Andy did his best to keep his faithful Old English Sheepdog, Fluff, off the couch, but the dog was stubborn, and unfortunately for the family, in the midst of his summer molt.

Most people liked his dog. Unfortunately, his brother Bob was not among them. "Andy, we have to share this cottage, but I spend most of my two weeks here getting the damned dog hair off my sweaters. Why can't you leave Fluff home?"

It is a toss-up as to which is more controversial: the right of a surviving spouse to use the cottage, or cat and dog fights. I refer not to the actual owners, but to the dissension between pet-loving cottage owners and pet-loathing cottage owners.

Some besotted owners simply cannot understand why everyone does not love the Fluffster. Such intelligence! Such playfulness! Such big brown eyes! Such stains on the carpet ....hmmm.

I really have no answer to the problem. Each family must craft its own compromise on the pet-presence problem. Some impose a fee on the pet owner. The money is used to pay a cleaning service to remove evidence of the four-legged offender. Especially if another owner is allergic to your pet, courtesy would dictate that you lodge the pooch at Club Kennel instead of the cottage. If another owner is not allergic, you have to decide whether your relationship with the other owner is more important than your relationship with the pet. A nontrivial question!

The Bottom Line on Cottage Sharing

The Golden Rule — the key to successful cottage sharing — is to *accommodate the reasonable desires of the other owners, and a couple of the unreasonable ones for good measure.* No schedule is perfect. No set of access rules is perfect. The family that works through these issues and expresses in its operating agreement the compromises attained through reasoned deliberation stands the best chance of happily sharing the cottage.

Chapter 14

RENTING THE COTTAGE

Cottages are expensive to keep. Even if there is no mortgage on the cottage, property taxes, maintenance expenses, and property insurance adds up to thousands of dollars each year.

Renting the cottage can be its salvation. If just one cottage owner is unable to easily afford his share of expenses, some families allow that owner to rent his allotted cottage time and retain the rental income. While this can be a good solution, I urge these families to consult with an accountant first, as renting will complicate the filing of federal and state income tax returns. Fairness dictates that the increase in expense caused by rental (for instance, higher costs for tax return preparation, property insurance, and cleaning service) should be borne by the owner who receives the rent. Unless the income it produces is significant, it might not be worth the hassle and administrative costs to rent the cottage.

For instance, assume Bob is posted overseas for two years. Although he will be unable to use his month at the cottage he still is obligated to pay his share of yearly costs. With the permission of his family (as expressed through the cottage operating agreement), Bob could rent his month to a friend and collect the rent personally. So long as Bob bears *all* expenses of the arrangement, and pays for any damage caused by the friend, it would seem an advantageous arrangement to all.

But while renting the cottage can be its salvation — saving co-owners from having to sell their shares, in some instances — renting also can create strains within a family, expose the family to liability and the cottage to damage, and complicate use and administration of the cottage.

It is surprising how complex something as seemingly simple as renting a cottage can be. By understanding these complexities you will be able to make an informed decision on whether to rent or not to rent, and how to go about it if you do. The following steps are crucial to successful cottage rental:

+ Confirm that rental is permitted under zoning and any restrictive covenants that govern your cottage.

+ Tell your insurance agent you will be renting the cottage and pay for increased insurance coverage if necessary.

+ Operate through an LLC or corporation.

+ Use a lease prepared or reviewed by an attorney.

+ Have a detailed contract with your rental management company (if you use one).

+ Offer to compensate the family member who manages your rentals or your relationship with the rental management company.

- Have a clear understanding of the true costs of rental:
  - Increased cost for preparation of federal and state income tax returns.
  - Cost of preparing and filing a sales tax return (if your state taxes cottage rental income).
  - Increased insurance cost.
  - Rental agency fees.
  - Legal costs (lease preparation, eviction).
  - Repair costs (tenants can be hard on a place).

Let's look at rental issues in greater depth.

Is Rental Permitted?

The first question is whether the cottage may be rented without violating the law or deed restrictions on the cottage.

Renting is viewed in some communities as a commercial activity. Almost all cottages are located in residential zoning districts. Unless your zoning ordinance permits rental, cottage owners may not *legally* rent their cottage. (To be sure, some owners chance it and rent the cottage anyway, but they run the risk that a disgruntled neighbor will turn them in, resulting in an embarrassing situation for the cottage owner and the renter.) Check with your local government to see what rental-related rules, if any, apply to your cottage.

Perhaps your cottage sits on a parcel created by a land developer. Developers often establish written rules (**restrictive covenants**) to limit how property may be developed and used. Before renting the cottage, review the title to your property to see if a restrictive covenant applies to your cottage, and if so, whether it prohibits renting the cottage. Even if the developer is long gone any neighbor may enforce the covenant against you.

Rental Operations

Cottages often are rented to friends, distant family, and acquaintances — in other words, people who probably value their relationship with you in addition to the opportunity to use your cottage. These are ideal renters: they're more likely than strangers to treasure the cottage, report damages, and abide cottage rules in general.

This is not to say that strangers don't make good tenants — the majority of time they do. But renting to the general public involves more oversight, and requires greater caution, than renting to your friends and acquaintances.

It is beyond the scope of this book to describe, in any depth, how to act like a landlord. Rental management is a complex business that involves a laundry list of duties: marketing the cottage, screening prospective tenants, handling deposits in accordance with state law, taking reservations, obtaining and using a lease form that meets the legal requirements of the state where the cottage is located, inspecting the cottage before the renters arrive and after they depart, seeing the cottage is maintained and cleaned properly, policing overcrowding, making sure linens and towels are provided, handling cancellations, collecting and remitting sales tax (if required by the state where your cottage is located), delivering and retrieving cottage keys, enforcing rules so renters are safe, making sure renters are respectful of the cottage and neighbors, and dealing with the liberation of items from the cottage by unscrupulous renters.

If you've decided to rent, you must choose whether to self-manage the cottage or to hire a rental management company. The former is likely to result in greater net income at the cost of a considerable amount of time and trouble for at least one of the cottage owners. The latter entrusts your cottage to a rental management company.

Resort areas are likely to have one or more rental property management companies that will take care of most all rental-related issues: they advertise and market cottages, secure tenants, obtain security deposits, have the tenants sign rental agreements, prepare the cottage for rental (or supervise a cleaning service hired for this purpose), show the tenants through the cottage and explain cottage rules, address problems that arise during the tenant's occupancy, inspect the cottage when the tenants depart, return the deposit to the tenant (minus payment for any damage), and prepare the cottage for the next occupant. In our area the property manager typically receives thirty percent of rental income.

Rental management companies are profit driven, so they may not screen prospective renters as aggressively as an owner might, be as vigilant about maintenance, or notice damaged or missing items. It is worth asking around to see if other cottage owners can recommend a good company.

Whether you rent the cottage yourself or use a rental management company, you should insist renters sign a lease that meets the legal requirements of your cottage's state. This businesslike step will minimize the possibility of misunderstandings and will help you collect from a tenant if something goes wrong. Although rental management companies may have a lease form, in my experience these forms leave much to be desired. Some do not meet the minimum legal requirements. I urge you to have a short-term lease drafted by a real estate attorney from the state where your cottage is located, or to have the rental company's standard rental agreement reviewed by an attorney for compliance with law. A landlord who directly, or indirectly through his cottage rental agent, violates tenant protection laws, however accidentally, is taking an unnecessary risk.

Your agreement with a rental management company also should be reduced to writing, and it should describe the company's responsibility and its compensation. For instance, is the company entitled to a fee if the renter cancels?

When discussing rental management you may find that the management company requires your cottage to be available for a minimum number of weeks each season, or to be available the best weeks of the season. This may preclude using a rental management company, particularly if you only want to rent the cottage for four weeks per year or less.

Who Is the Landlord?

Another question when deciding to rent is whether it is a family activity or an individual activity. In the former case, the company will act as landlord. The company will decide which weeks will be rented, make the rental arrangements, and collect the rents. If it is an individual activity, as when Bob rented his month to a friend, the individual co-owner assumes responsibility for the arrangement, but the family remains at some risk if the renter suffers a personal injury. Provided the rental is conducted through the cottage LLC, however, each owner's personal assets are protected by the LLC's liability shield.

Compensate a Family Manager

The burden of property management is heavy and often falls upon the sibling who lives closest to the cottage. Human nature being what it is, a "property manager" sibling who is not adequately rewarded for his or her service can feel used, which often leads to unhappy sibling relations and a cottage crisis. It is wise to offer compensation to the family member who takes on the burden of rental management. Some will accept the offer; for others, the gesture is sufficient compensation.

Liability

You become a landlord when you take money from a non-owner for the use of the cottage, and when that happens many laws suddenly come into play. You should be aware of these laws — at least generally — to protect yourself and the cottage.

Because the law requires a landlord to maintain the rental property in a reasonably safe condition, you are liable for personal injury or property damage caused by any unsafe condition. For example, assume the cottage has a lovely loft. Now imagine a renter named Ralph crashes through its flimsy railing and winds up paralyzed. To make matters worse everybody in your family knew the railing was bad, but nobody got around to fixing it. Ralph is certain to sue. At best, your insurance will pay his claim in full. At worst, Ralph will levy against the cottage, and possibly against the personal assets of each owner to satisfy his judgment.

There are a number of steps you should take to prevent yourself and your cottage from incidents like this and the claims that result. These include:

Proper maintenance: To state the obvious: don't rent the cottage in an unsafe condition. If there is something that makes the cottage unsafe to a reasonable person, then you should fix it before you allow the renter to take possession. Although docks, stairs, and watercraft cause many injuries, as long as they are in good condition you will not be liable to the tenant. These dangers are considered "open and obvious" to the renters, who assume the risk for their use.

INSURANCE: Your homeowner's insurance policy is the first line of defense if a renter is injured despite your good maintenance. Premiums for cottage policies are computed on the assumption that the cottage won't be rented. Renting the cottage increases the chances of a claim so insurance companies charge higher premiums to cover this higher risk. *It is imperative you disclose to your insurance agent your intention to rent the cottage even if you know it will increase your insurance expense.* Why? Because insurance companies are not charities. They seek to preserve their assets by denying claims. Homeowner's insurance policies typically exclude from coverage claims that arise if the property is rented. Therefore, even though you pay a premium for a homeowner's policy, the insurance company is not obligated to pay claims arising from rental activity. It is stupid to game the system.

I explained earlier that a limited liability company protects the assets of the *owners* of the company from creditor claims. A limited liability company does not, however, protect the assets of the *company* from these claims. This is why it is so important to have proper insurance if the cottage will be rented.

LIMITING THE LIABILITY OF OWNERS TO RENTERS: Assume that Ralph, who fell through the loft railing, won a $1.5 million judgment and your insurance policy paid its $500,000 limit. Ralph is owed $1 million after collecting from your insurance company. Assume the cottage is worth $600,000. Ralph can and will ask the sheriff to sell your cottage to satisfy his judgment. He will be owed $400,000 after he collects his $600,000 from the sale. If you own the cottage through a limited liability company or a corporation Ralph is out of luck: he will not be able to collect the $400,000 from you. This is what is meant by limited liability.

If you owned the cottage directly or through a partnership, Ralph may levy on the assets of each of the cottage's owners until his judgment is satisfied. Ralph has the privilege of deciding which of the cottage owners to pursue (and naturally, he would pick the richest). After paying the $400,000 to Ralph, the unlucky, formerly rich owner could then sue the other owners for reimbursement. If the cottage is owned by a trust, Ralph will sue to collect his $400,000 from the trustee.

The lessons here are to make sure you have adequate insurance *and to own your cottage through a limited liability company or a corporation.*

More complex strategies afford the cottage and you even greater protection from creditor claims. One recognized asset-protection strategy is for the cottage LLC to establish a second limited liability company ("Rental LLC"). In this arrangement Cottage LLC leases the cottage to Rental LLC. The lease requires Rental LLC to maintain the cottage. Rental LLC buys commercial insurance and leases the cottage to your tenants. The cottage (owned

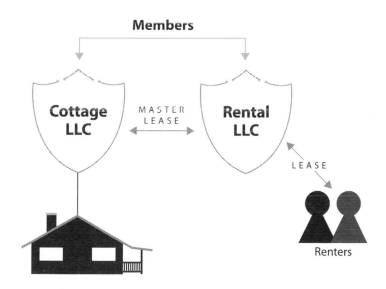

ESTABLISH A SECOND LIMITED LIABILTY COMPANY

by Cottage LLC) is not subject to creditor claims if Rental LLC is properly capitalized and maintained.

A variation on this strategy is for the family to form Rental LLC instead of causing Cottage LLC to form Rental LLC.

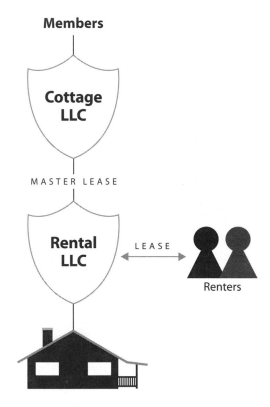

CASE LLC FORMS A RENTAL LLC

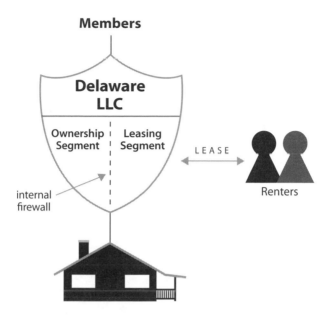

DELAWARE LLC OPTION

A third variation is to take advantage of a special provision in the laws of some states (notably Delaware) that permits two quasi-entities to exist within one LLC, sometimes called a "series LLC" or a "cell LLC." The operating agreement for the company may segregate the ownership and leasing activity of the company, creating an internal firewall between each cell that protects the ownership side of the LLC from liability arising from the leasing side's rental activities.

Creating a Cottage Legacy

Chapter 15

MINIMIZING THE
FEDERAL TAX BITE

One of the most serious impediments to passing a cottage from generation to generation is the estate tax — something that can ruin even the finest cottage succession plan. If the law does not change, starting in 2011, many estates may suffer tax bills so high that the family cottage will have to be sold to pay the levy.

Thankfully, under current tax law, it is possible to make annual tax-free gifts of your interest in the cottage to your descendants, so that, over a period of years you have transferred the entire cottage out of your estate (and away from those deadly taxes). But using this gift exemption takes some finesse. You should carefully follow the advice of your professional advisors to avoid an unnecessary dispute with the IRS.

Death, Taxes, and Cottages

The federal government will tax your estate if you die rich enough. Because the estate tax is one of Washington's favorite political footballs, the amount that makes you "rich enough" has moved up and down over the years.

The Economic Growth and Tax Relief Reconciliation Act of 2001 was one of the first acts George W. Bush signed as president, delivering (sort of) on his campaign promise to completely repeal the estate tax. This act increased the estate exclusion amount (the value exempt from tax) and decreased estate tax rates. The act also provided a bizarre situation: for people "lucky" enough (or rather, the heirs of people so fortunate) to die in 2010, estates will not be taxed no matter how large they are. Here is a summary of the estate tax as it stands in 2007:

Estate Tax

Year of Death	Exclusion Amount	Rate of Tax over Exclusion Amount
2007-2008	$2,000,000	up to 45%
2009	$3,500,000	up to 45%
2010	unlimited	no estate tax
2011	**$1,000,000**	**up to 55%**

A close reading of this table leads one to the conclusion that December 2010, is a poor month to be a wealthy person on life support.

Why, you may wonder, would there be no estate tax on December 31, 2010, and a potentially huge tax for the person who dies one day later? The answer lies in the Byrd Amendment, a Senate procedural rule that provides that no tax law can have effect for more than ten years without a vote of sixty senators. Since 2001, Republicans have lacked sufficient votes to override the Byrd Amendment and make the estate tax repeal permanent, so we are left with an estate tax table that only could have been designed in Washington.

The bizarre rate table seriously complicates tax planning for cottage owners. Because the focus of this book is cottage succession planning, not tax planning, I will not attempt to offer estate tax saving strategies here. For that, I encourage you to consult with a qualified estate tax attorney, accountant, or financial planner. I will, however, discuss some cottage-specific planning considerations.

Using annual exclusion gifts to transfer the cottage tax free

Were there no gift tax, taxpayers could bypass the estate tax by giving away all property while on their deathbeds. Federal law prevents this end run by imposing a gift tax on most transfers — those over a certain value — made while the donor is alive.

An important exception to the gift tax allows you to make an annual tax-free gift to any person. In 2007, every adult is free to give away the equivalent of $12,000 per year, per person, and no one pays any taxes. These "exclusion gifts" are a very common estate planning tool because they allow wealth to be transferred from one generation to the next free of any form of tax   the wealth is no longer part of an estate, and such gifts are not treated as taxable income for recipients. For couples, each spouse is entitled to this amount, which means that together a married couple may give up to $24,000 per year per person to an unlimited number of persons, whether a child, grandchild, niece, nephew, or friend.

How can exclusion gifts be used in cottage succession plans? Let's assume Mary and John own a cottage worth $1 million, a home worth $500,000, and $1 million in investments. They want to avoid estate tax and pass the cottage on to their three children. They've set up estate planning trusts to minimize the tax bite. But, if they both die after 2010, that still leaves $500,000 vulnerable to estate tax. Since they have sufficient pension and Social Security income, along with excellent medical and long-term-care insurance, Mary and John decide to make $12,000 annual gifts to their children each year, until they've reduced the size of their combined taxable estates to $2 million.

John's preferred approach is to give interests in the cottage to his children. This satisfies his objective of conserving cash for a rainy day and advances his goal of transferring the cottage to his children. Aware of the problems of tenancy in common, he proposes this plan:

1. John and Mary will deed the cottage to a new cottage limited liability company.

2. Fifty percent of the company membership units will be issued to John's trust and fifty percent to Mary's trust.

3. John, as trustee of his trust, will withdraw from his trust membership interests worth $12,000. He will give one of these $12,000 interests to each of his children each year. Mary will do the same.

4. John and Mary will file an IRS Form 709 annually, reporting these gifts by April 15.

5. In fourteen years they will have transferred the cottage to their children.

Problem solved, right?

Maybe, maybe not. A tax planning strategy such as this must be evaluated for risk. Will the IRS challenge the plan? Perhaps. If the plan comes unraveled after John and Mary's death, how do they feel about putting their heirs into a fight with the Internal Revenue Service?

Some plans have little risk, some have a lot. Some taxpayers so hate the idea of paying taxes that they will assume this risk; meanwhile, others will pay taxes even if they possess good arguments for avoiding them, just to avoid any possibility of a fight.

Recent Tax Court decisions require John and Mary to implement their plan carefully. Let's consider John's plan. Section 2503 of Internal Revenue Code permits a taxpayer to make *qualified* gifts of $12,000 per person per year with no tax impact. A *qualified* gift meets two tests:

TEST 1: The taxpayer must transfer a "present interest" to the donee.

TEST 2: The taxpayer may not retain an interest in the asset transferred.

A gift that flunks either test will be included in the taxpayer's estate even if the taxpayer thinks he has given the property away. The stakes are significant. If the IRS invalidates John's plan, John or Mary's estate will incur a $200,000 tax that could have been avoided with proper gift planning. The tax bill might compel the sale of the cottage to pay the tax — a cottage succession planning disaster.

Does John's plan meet Test 1 and Test 2? If we cannot confidently say yes, then John and Mary will have to decide if the reward for John's plan (passing the cottage to their children free of estate tax) outweighs its risk (litigation with the IRS and a possible $200,000 tax).

Test 1 requires John and Mary to make a gift of a "present interest" in property. A present interest is one that takes effect immediately. One would think that a gift of an interest in John and Mary's cottage LLC qualifies easily because John and Mary no longer own the membership unit transferred to one of their children. They cannot get it back. Surely their gift of a membership interest is a present interest?

Not exactly. Let's explore a court case involving this very question.

Test 1: The Hackls and the present interest requirement.

Albert Hackl, a mechanical engineer, grew the annual sales of a company that manufactured scholastic and motivational rewards from $18 million (in 1965) to $265 million (in 1995). On retirement he sold his stock to the company's retirement plan for millions, much of which he invested in publicly-traded stock. Deciding to diversify his portfolio into real estate, Albert set up Treeco LLC, a limited liability company, and contributed tree farms worth $4.5 million plus $8 million in other assets to the company. Albert and his wife, Christine, owned all of the membership units of Treeco through their estate planning trusts.

Like our John, Albert hit upon a plan to use the annual gift tax exclusion (at the time, $10,000) to reduce the size of his and his wife's taxable estates, thereby saving estate tax. In 1995, Albert and Christine gave separate membership interests in Treeco worth $10,000 to each of their eight children. They also gave membership interests to their children's spouses, so that the 1995 gifts removed $320,000 from Albert and Christine's combined estates. The Hackls accelerated their gifting program in 1996 by adding gifts to trusts established for each of their twenty-five grandchildren, each of whom, like their parents, received $20,000 each. The 1996 gifts were valued at $820,000.

The Hackls reported the 1996 gifts to the IRS, which had until April 15, 2000, to challenge the gifts. Imagine the couple's disappointment when, on April 14, 2000, the IRS notified them that their 1996 gifts were being disqualified because they were not gifts of a "present interest."

The Hackls took the IRS to Tax Court, where the government argued that, based upon prior case rulings, the Hackls failed to prove that their children, children's spouses, and grandchildren's trusts enjoyed a "substantial present economic benefit by reason of use, possession, or enjoyment of either the property itself or income from the property." The IRS argued that these descendants had not substantially benefited, economically, from the LLC membership shares they'd received.

The Hackls, meanwhile, argued that the membership interests given to their descendants were identical to their own membership interests. The court did not dispute this assertion. On paper each descendant's membership interest was the same as the interests owned by the Hackls.

The Hackls would have won their case had the court's analysis stopped here. The court, however, did not stop. Instead it closely analyzed the Treeco operating agreement. The judge noted that Albert, as the company's manager, retained three key powers: the power to decide whether a member could receive a capital distribution from the company, the power to allow a member to withdraw from the company, and the power to decide whether a member could sell his or her units to a third party. These retained powers, the court ruled, prevented each descendant from unilaterally obtaining the economic benefits of ownership of units in Treeco. This, combined with the fact that Treeco was not expected to distribute income to its owners for many years, allowed the court to find that the Hackl gifts were not present interests, and hence were not eligible for the $10,000 per person per year exclusion from gift tax.

The tax bill resulting from this loss was more than $600,000, so (unsurprisingly) the Hackls invested in an appeal. The appellate court, in approving the Tax Court's reasoning and ruling against the Hackls, said:

> The Hackls protest that Treeco is set up like any other limited liability corporation and that its restrictions on the alienability of its shares are common in closely held companies. While that may be true, the fact that other companies operate this way does not mean that shares in such companies should automatically be considered present interests for purposes of the gift tax exclusion. As we have previously said, Internal Revenue Code provisions dealing with exclusions are matters of legislative grace that must be narrowly construed. [citation omitted] The onus is on the taxpayers to show that their transfers qualify for the gift tax exclusion, a burden the Hackls have not met.

Does this ruling mean that John shouldn't implement a gifting program? Not necessarily. These decisions illustrate, however, that John's plan contains risk, and that it will fail if the cottage LLC's operating agreement isn't properly written.

How might John and Mary draft a successful operating agreement? The Hackl case provides the best example of what to avoid:

- Company management was vested solely in Albert.

- Albert designated himself as manager for life.

- Albert had power to appoint a successor during his lifetime or in his last will and testament.

- Albert controlled all financial distributions.

* Members couldn't exit the company without Albert's approval, who had authority to set the price and terms for sale of the membership interests.

* A member could not transfer his interest in any way (including selling) without Albert's consent, which would be given or withheld in Albert's sole discretion.

* Albert determined whether the company could be dissolved.

Based on these "don'ts," how, then, should we write John and Mary's cottage operating agreement so they may legally gift company interests to their children?

First, we want to ensure that each child gained a present and substantial economic benefit from their interest in the cottage limited liability company. Unlike the Treeco operating agreement, which gave the children no right to use the tree farm property (they probably wouldn't have wanted it anyway), our operating agreement will give each child a substantial right: the right to use the family cottage. People pay hundreds and even thousands of dollars for a week at somebody else's cottage. By itself, the right to use John and Mary's cottage should persuade a court that each child's interest is both present and substantial.

The powers Albert Hackl retained clearly bothered both courts that considered his case. John and Mary's cottage operating agreement should not grant dictatorial authority to their company's manager. Instead, John and Mary's operating agreement could give their children a say in selection of the manager, in whether the company should be dissolved, and in other matters.

The Tax Court also was troubled by the fact that the Hackl children received something they could not sell without Albert's permission. I would advise John and Mary to include a put option in their operating agreement. The put option, discussed in Chapter 11, allows any member to *force* the company to buy them out. In addition, the operating agreement would permit John and Mary's descendants to sell their interest in the company both within and outside the family, after giving the company and/or certain members first right of purchase.

Because tax law constantly evolves though legislation, IRS interpretation, and litigation, it is not necessarily possible to guarantee a taxpayer's plan will succeed. The more aggressive the taxpayer's position, the more likely it will attract an IRS challenge. That said, under current law, I believe that if John and Mary's cottage LLC operating agreement contains the provisions described here, John's gifting plan will work — but only if it satisfies the additional requirements described below.

Test 2: The Tehans and the retained interest problem.

Wouldn't it be great to give something away (avoiding estate tax), yet still be able to enjoy it for the rest of your life?

You're right — it would be great. But unfortunately, it's too good to be true.

Timothy Tehan, who owned a condominium unit in Chevy Chase, Maryland, worried about estate taxes (just like our John and Mary), so he decided to give the condo to his children. Timothy's attorney prepared an agreement and series of deeds to implement a gifting program. Timothy and his children signed the agreement, following which Timothy transferred a four and one-half percent interest in the property to each of his eight children. The family repeated the process in the succeeding two years, at the end of which Timothy's children owned 100 percent of the condo.

The agreement provided that Timothy could live in the condo for the rest of his life, that he would not have to pay rent to his children, and prevented Timothy's children from selling their interests in the condo without first offering the interest to Timothy. Under the agreement Timothy was required to pay the mortgage, condo assessment, property taxes, insurance, and maintenance costs so long as he lived in the unit.

Timothy died two months after he completed his gifting program. From the date of the first deed until he died, Timothy was the sole occupant of the condo and paid all associated expenses but no rent. His children sold the condo after his death.

The IRS argued this gifting program was invalid because Timothy effectively owned an interest in the condo even though on paper it did not appear so. The court agreed with the IRS and included the condo's full value in Timothy's taxable estate.

Timothy's plan probably would have worked if he had vacated the condo after completing his gifting program. Doing so would have proved he did not retain a veiled lifetime interest in the property. Timothy also could have rescued the plan by paying his children the fair market rental value of the condo.

Implicitly, the court ruled that Timothy could not have it both ways: either he really gave up his interest in the condo by moving out or paying fair market rent (in which case the condo would not be part of his taxable estate) or he did not really give up his interest in the condo (in which case the "gifts" he made to his children would be ignored).

Timothy's case offers an important planning pointer to John and Mary. *In addition to having a properly drafted operating agreement, John and Mary either must stop using the family cottage (unlikely and undesirable) or pay a fair market rent to the company for their use of the cottage.* The rent they pay should be reported as company income on the IRS Form 1065 that the company already is filing in order to claim its real property tax deduction. The amount of rent should be the same a stranger would pay for the type of use that John and Mary enjoyed.

Most of my clients do not object to paying rent to the family company. After all, the money really is going to their children. The act of paying rent demonstrates to the IRS the *bona fide* nature of the membership transfer, and in all likelihood will persuade the IRS to deploy its enforcement resources against a family that has not observed the requisite formalities.

The Price Tag on Cottage Units

If you can meet Tests 1 and 2, you will be able to start your gifting program once you can put a value on each cottage LLC membership unit.

And there's the rub: how much *is* a unit of LLC ownership worth? That's a good question. How much would *you* pay a stranger for a twenty-five percent interest in his cottage worth $240,000? Would you pay $60,000, a quarter of its retail value? No, I wouldn't either. For one thing, I'd have to share the cottage with strangers; that isn't very appealing. And, if the cottage were held in a limited liability company, in all probability my quarter interest would not be sufficient to permit me to exert meaningful control over company operations. I would be at the mercy of the seventy-five percent owner. Not to mention, cottage operating agreements often devalue LLC shares, marking down the cottage's street value by twenty percent to fifty percent to discourage relatives from cashing in shares (see Chapter 11).

Nonetheless, were I *really* interested in the cottage, I might pay perhaps $40,000 or $45,000 for the quarter interest, especially if I had some written assurances concerning my rights. The lower price reflects the difficulty the seller would have in persuading me to buy his interest — I would be worried about how I'd be treated as a minority owner and would insist on a bargain rate.

The price assigned to LLC shares makes a big difference in cottage gifting programs. The lower the value, the quicker the transfer. For example, assume John and Mary's $1 million cottage has 500 LLC membership shares. Without discounting the cottage's street value at all, it would take John and Mary fourteen years to give all ownership interest in the cottage LLC to their three children. However, by discounting the cottage's value by forty percent, they'd be done in just nine years:

How Discounts Benefit Gifting Programs

Discount	0%	10%	20%	30%	40%
Value/unit	$2,000	$1,800	$1,600	$1,400	$1,200
Units given/year	6.0	6.7	7.5	8.6	10.0
Year 1	36	40	45	51.4	60
Year 2	36	40	45	51.4	60
Year 3	36	40	45	51.4	60
Year 4	36	40	45	51.4	60
Year 5	36	40	45	51.4	60
Year 6	36	40	45	51.4	60
Year 7	36	40	45	51.4	60
Year 8	36	40	45	51.4	60
Year 9	36	40	45	51.4	20
Year 10	36	40	45	37.2	
Year 11	36	40	45		
Year 12	36	40	5		
Year 13	36	20			
Year 14	32				
Units given away	500	500	500	500	500

The IRS hates valuation discounts and has developed a number of theories as to why they may not be claimed in connection with gifts of interests in family limited partnerships, corporations, and limited liability companies. You should not claim a valuation discount in connection with a gift program unless you fully understand the audit and litigation risks involved. A qualified lawyer or accountant can explain these risks to you. If you go down this road, it would be wise to mind the tax planning maxim that "Pigs get fat, hogs get slaughtered."

Appraisals and IRS Reporting

How do we know John and Mary's cottage is worth $1 million? It certainly would improve their gift program if they underestimate the value of the cottage, but we really can't expect the IRS to take John and Mary's word for it. Perhaps they could use their property tax assessment? After all, tax assessors work for the government. The IRS is part of the government. So John and Mary can use their tax assessment to determine the value of their cottage for gift tax purposes, right?

Wrong. The IRS does not accept values set by tax assessors for estate or gift tax purposes. The IRS insists upon a formal current appraisal by a qualified appraiser. This appraisal is attached to IRS Form 709, which is used by John and Mary to report their gifts. The IRS generally considers an appraisal to be current if it's prepared within six months of the date of the gift, so a good method is to have the appraisal prepared in the last quarter of the year (e.g. October through December). This allows you to use the appraisal to value gifts made in that year and in the first three months of the following tax year.

Why should John and Mary bother to report their $12,000 exclusion gifts to the IRS? The gifts are tax-exempt, after all, and reporting them might attract an audit.

The answer is that the IRS has only three years from April 15 of the year after the gift was made to challenge the gift. Once that date passes, and provided your IRS Form 709 adequately discloses certain information — the number of LLC units and percentage of ownership transferred, names and relationships of recipients, and an appraisal and information on valuation discounts (if applicable) — then years later, the IRS can't challenge the values reported on the Form 709. Once the challenge date passes, John and Mary may relax, content in the knowledge that John's estate tax saving plan succeeded.

Chapter 16

THE ULTIMATE GIFT: A COTTAGE ENDOWMENT

Cottage operating expenses — from taxes and insurance to repairs and upgrades — are a burden to owners. And they definitely will be a burden to most heirs. Many of my clients are deeply worried that their heirs, collectively, won't be able to afford to keep the cottage because of the thousands in annual expenses it demands. Others are concerned that their less affluent children, unable to pay their shares on time (or at all), will lose their places at the cottage to wealthier siblings.

These are persistent and valid concerns among cottage founders. And luckily, for those of you with enough capital, there is a financial solution to address this worry — an **endowment,** which is a fund dedicated to paying future cottage expenses. I borrow the term endowment because of the fund's similarity to the permanent endowments established by universities, hospitals, boarding schools, community foundations, and other not-for-profit organizations.

What Is an Endowment?

The key feature of an endowment is that access to the fund's principal is restricted, but its income and gains are used to pay the costs of keeping the cottage in your family. For instance, if a family established a $300,000 cottage endowment and the fund earned five percent, the $15,000 in annual income would be available to pay property taxes, insurance, and maintenance expenses. Even if the annual income did not pay all expenses of the cottage, the $15,000 contribution would greatly ease the financial burden of cottage ownership on the heirs.

While all heirs benefit from the endowment, less affluent heirs, for whom cottage expenses are especially burdensome, usually are most grateful for the financial relief afforded by the endowment.

How Is an Endowment Established?

Cottage owners who opt for an endowment must decide when to fund it. There are a variety of options. Among them:

ESTATES: If there is but a single cottage owner, or a couple, these owners ordinarily defer funding the endowment until they have died. In other words, the endowment comes from their estate. The estate planning document (a revocable or irrevocable trust) used to manage the cottage endowment will instruct how much money the trustee must allocate to the endowment (a dollar amount or a percentage of the distributable assets), whether and when principal of the trust fund may be distributed to the company, and the circumstances that cause the trust to terminate.

CO-OWNERS: Cottages with multiple owners (siblings, cousins, friends) have a wider range of alternatives. If the owners have sufficient resources, they might fund the endowment immediately. More frequently, however, the owners decide to fund the endowment gradually through a series of annual assessments.

Sometimes, perhaps because of limited means, these co-owners pledge among themselves to fund the endowment when each dies. The skeptical reader may wonder how this works. If the co-owner reneges on his commitment, what recourse does one have? The solution is for each co-owner to make a written commitment to contribute a certain amount to the endowment at that owner's death. This commitment might be in the form of an **estate promissory note**. The point is to create an arrangement that gives the company a legally enforceable right to collect from each owner or from that owner's estate a proportionate contribution to the company's endowment. If, after the person dies, the commitment is not honored by that individual's heirs, the call option is triggered, resulting in the involuntary termination of the decedent's interest in the company at the discount specified in the operating agreement.

LIFE INSURANCE: Life insurance may be used to fund the endowment. By way of example, if a sixty-five-year-old owner commits to transfer $100,000 to the family cottage LLC at his death, the owner may buy a policy and name the company as the policy death beneficiary. When the person dies, the death benefit satisfies the decedent's obligations to the company under the subscription agreement or the estate promissory note. The foregoing assumes the person's health is such that he or she can purchase life insurance.

Another possibility is for children to purchase an insurance policy on the lives of their parents with the proceeds to be used to fund a cottage endowment.

SECOND-TO-DIE LIFE INSURANCE: This is what it sounds like — insurance that pays out on the death of two insured persons. Many estate plans are designed to defer estate tax until the second spouse dies. Second-to-die life insurance originally was developed to generate the funds needed to pay estate tax at the second spouse's death. Since two lives are being insured simultaneously this increases the odds that at least one of the persons will live past the predicted date of death of either person. As a result, the premiums for second-to-die life insurance are relatively low when compared to the cost of insuring a single life. Second-to-die insurance is a relatively inexpensive way to create a cottage endowment.

Irrevocable Life Insurance Trust: Life insurance may be used in more sophisticated ways to fund the endowment. A common estate planning tool is the irrevocable life insurance trust (ILIT). This is a trust whose only asset is one or more life insurance policies. The trust determines how the death benefit is distributed. The key benefit of an ILIT is that the death benefit of a life insurance policy payable to ILIT is not subject to estate tax. An ILIT funded by a regular or second-to-die life insurance policy is an excellent tool to create and manage a cottage endowment.

Size of Endowment

The ideal endowment is one large enough to generate enough income to pay the reasonably foreseeable cottage expenses in perpetuity. If the endowment is large enough, no heir will ever have to pay for the privilege of using the cottage. This is a wonderful gift to one's descendants.

The amount of money that would be required for this perfect endowment depends upon:

- The projected annual cottage expenses

- The assumed return on invested funds

- The inflation rate

- The income tax rate

We will examine each of these separately:

Projected expenses: The annual cost to maintain the cottage probably is the easiest to estimate, especially for families that have owned their cottage for many years. Costs include annual fees for utilities, any mortgages, insurance, taxes, and routine maintenance. Be sure to factor in savings for large, periodic expenses, such as roofs or major appliances.

Projected rate of return and inflation rate: It is difficult to predict the future's return on invested funds and the inflation rate. Lacking a crystal ball that works, your best bet is to look at history as a guide. Since 1926, the average appreciation rate for the Standard and Poors 500 stock index has been twelve percent, and the average rate of return for bonds is six and one-half percent. An endowment portfolio is likely to be a blend of these investments. The annual inflation rate over the last seventy years has averaged four percent.

Projected income tax rate: Because endowment fund income is taxed to individual LLC members, a true self-funding endowment will distribute enough cash to make up for each heir's endowment-related income tax liability.

How Do Heirs Feel about an Endowment?

As the old saying goes, "Where you stand depends upon where you sit."

Heirs who want to keep the cottage in the family and heirs with children often will be enthusiastic about an endowment. Childless heirs or heirs who are ambivalent about the cottage sometimes greet the idea of an endowment with less enthusiasm. Heirs with few financial resources may view the endowment in one of two ways: if they really want the right to use the cottage, they may like the endowment because it will permit them to remain an owner.

If, on the other hand, they are not wedded to the cottage, they may resent having a part of their inheritance tied up in an endowment. Reconciling disparate feelings about the endowment can be a great challenge for parents planning their estates. I propose some polite responses for the parent whose intention to establish a cottage endowment is challenged by a child:

"While I appreciate your concern, I believe that establishing the endowment is in the best interest of *all* of my children."

"I would be happy to exclude you from the cottage, and will attempt to compensate you with other assets from my estate."

"The cottage operating agreement allows you to receive a share of the endowment by exercising your put option."

The End of the Endowment

In states that retain the **rule against perpetuities**, endowments must terminate in about ninety years. Although endowments established in states that do not follow the rule against perpetuities and endowments established within the cottage LLC theoretically need never terminate, the document that creates the endowment should describe the circumstances under which the endowment ends.

For instance, if one branch bought out all of the other branches, does the endowment continue or is it distributed among the branches? Families that are especially keen on perpetuating the cottage might keep the endowment in place. The burden of maintaining a very small endowment may not be worth the trouble, so I recommend a clause that terminates the endowment if it falls below a specified size.

Clauses that describe the termination of the endowment typically provide that the money will be divided among either the cottage owners in proportion to the ownership percentage held by each, or among all descendants without regard to the participation in the cottage. Founders also might specify that a favorite charity receive the endowment when it ends.

How Is an Endowment Used?

A cottage endowment is not regulated. This means founders may write provisions into a trust or operating agreement that reflect the way they wish the endowment to be maintained and spent.

To simplify bookkeeping, the cottage endowment might authorize the trustee or LLC to expend all endowment net income and capital gain each year without regard to the underlying inflation or deflation rate. Families that want to ensure the endowment's purchasing power, however, might require the trustee or company to adjust for inflation or deflation using the Consumer Price Index.

A key decision in establishing a cottage endowment is whether the principal may be invaded, and if so, for what purpose. Invasion might be acceptable if the money is used to pay off an exiting member or to make emergency repairs. Some families establish the endowment *knowing* the principal will be tapped annually to help pay cottage operating expenses. These founders accept that the endowment eventually will disappear, at which time, if expenses aren't manageable, either some of their descendants will buy out others or the cottage will be sold outside the family.

How Is an Endowment Managed?

The persons who establish the endowment may choose to have it managed within the company or by an outside manager. The distinction is important.

If the endowment is managed by the company, members or managers must make endowment investment decisions. Founders skeptical of the family's investment expertise or who would prefer independent management (perhaps to give heirs one less thing to do — or to debate), may stipulate in their estate plans that the endowment will be established as a trust fund, and the trustee will continue to invest and administer the trust for the benefit of the company. A bank-trusteed endowment is a ready-made solution.

Endowments Managed by LLC

Recall that limited liability companies are managed by members or managers. A member-managed LLC is a direct democracy because each member votes on each administrative matter. Allowing all members to participate in administration of the cottage endowment will be difficult in all but the smallest and most harmonious member-managed companies.

Most family limited liability companies are manager-managed. The managers initially may be all of the owners (in which case it looks a lot like a member-managed company), but as the generational wheel turns, the managers become a mere subset of the owners. Power is concentrated in these managers who oversee the operation of the company for the benefit of all members.

Some companies, whether manager-based or member-based, designate one of their number to serve as the "investment manager." The investment manager establishes an investment account in the name of the company, directs the investment, and reports financial status periodically to managers or members. The members or other managers decide the degree to which they are comfortable delegating their authority to the investment manager and may establish investment guidelines to follow. Conservative families might require the endowment to be invested only in government securities or certificates of deposit. Families concerned with maintaining the purchasing power of the endowment might establish investment guidelines, such as half of the portfolio in stocks and half in high-grade bonds.

Endowments Managed by a Trust Company

Another approach is for the company to appoint a bank trust department or a brokerage firm to manage the endowment. This is an excellent solution in that it shifts the burden of investment management outside the family to professional money managers. Unlike the trust-based endowment, the company retains ultimate control of the endowment and may discharge the outside investment firm if unsatisfied with its performance.

It is more complicated to establish a trust that pours money into a cottage LLC than to simply allow the cottage LLC to manage the money. So why would anyone consider a trust? One reason is a concern on the part of founders that heirs will not manage the endowment well, or as well as the institution selected by the founders. A second reason is that the founders seek to make cottage ownership as effortless as possible for the heirs by eliminating the burden of money management.

Income Tax Implications of Endowment

Although there will be no trust-level tax as long as all of the income is distributed to the cottage LLC, income of a trust must be disclosed to the Internal Revenue Service on an informational return (Form 1041). The trust will deliver a statement (Form K-1) to the limited liability company.

Recall, however, that limited liability companies normally are pass-through entities, not independent taxpayers. As a result, the company will give each of its owners another Form K-1 to reflect their proportionate share of trust/LLC income. Each heir will report this income to the IRS on Form 1040 and will be taxed on it.

So, if the endowment earned $15,000 and the cottage LLC had three equal owners, each would end up reporting $5,000 of additional income on their Form 1040 return.

The cottage endowment is an excellent way for families with sufficient resources to remove the financial burden of cottage ownership from future generations. A sufficient endowment will permit descendants to focus upon the enjoyment, not the management, of the cottage.

Even if you cannot fully endow a cottage, a modest endowment might enable the heirs to retain the cottage for a longer time and to avoid the need to rent the cottage to generate revenue. The endowment is especially helpful to the least affluent descendants.

CONCLUSION

Four out of five cottage owners say they wish to pass along this family treasure to future generations. They envision their children, grandchildren, great-grandchildren and subsequent generations bonded together by this single place, a place where descendants leave sandy footprints or build fires together and share hot chocolate as it snows. Leaving a cottage to descendants consecrates a family. It gives the entire family, throughout time, a place to gather and feel as one.

A cottage succession plan based on a limited liability company is the surest way achieve that dream. But you have to act, and the sooner the better.

Unfortunately, more than half of Americans don't have wills, including one of three persons with estates valued at more than $10 million. A 2007 survey disclosed that one in ten of those without a will said they didn't really want to think about dying or being incapacitated. Another ten percent just weren't sure how to go about it. Many others had the best intentions in the world, but didn't start or, even sadder, finish it on time.

If you do not have an estate plan the government will decide who gets what — including your cottage. Normally, your cottage will be split equally among heirs as tenants in common, which we all know means "trouble is coming." It sets the stage for family division, not lasting family unity.

Consider how widespread the potential for family strife is: there are more than 5.2 million vacation homes in the United States, and cottage ownership is increasing faster than private home ownership (the number of cottages increased by thirteen percent in the 1990s). Combine these facts with the tremendous increase in the values of individual second homes, add the fact that over eighty percent of cottages are owned free and clear, and you have an equation for heartache on a large scale.

Here is why: rapidly increasing cottage values, together with the fact that most are owned free and clear of mortgage debt, means the cottage often represents a substantial part of an owner's estate. This sets the stage for a tug-of-war between heirs of modest means (who may be counting on their share of the value of the cottage to pay debts, put their kids through college, or improve their lifestyle) and heirs who have been financially successful (to whom the prospect of using the cottage is more desirable than its cash value).

How many heirs will play tug of war over the family cottage? Will yours be among them? Wouldn't it make you happy to know that your descendants will be able to share the cottage into the future?

The surest way to avoid this conflict is to immediately discover if more than one of your children wants to inherit the cottage, and if so, set in motion a cottage succession plan. Do not put it off until tomorrow.

I remind my clients that a cottage plan is fluid and flexible. This is critical to keep in mind. A plan can change. It doesn't have to be perfect. The important thing is to have a plan in place. You can tinker with it as time goes by. Do not let perfection be the enemy of the perfectly adequate.

Start your plan today. If your children or grandchildren express interest in owning the cottage, then begin, step by step, to build a succession plan that will meet future challenges. With two simple steps — talking to your heirs and using the principles described in this book — you will set in motion a cottage succession plan that keeps the cottage in your bloodline, minimizes family fractures, shields your descendants from liability, and virtually eliminates the possibility of a forced sale of your treasured cottage.

You will be ensuring that your children, grandchildren, and great-grandchildren will always have a collective place to call home, a place where your portrait can look down, happily, from the mantle, decade after decade.

GLOSSARY

Where required by the context these definitions are specific to cottage succession planning.

Admission agreement: an agreement by which a potential member of a cottage LLC accepts that his or her relationship to the company (hence to the cottage) is governed by the LLC's operating agreement.

Appraiser: a professional person, typically licensed by a state, who is trained to give a written opinion as to the value of real property. An appraiser prepares an appraisal that may be used to establish the value of a cottage in connection with the sale and purchase of a membership interest in a cottage LLC.

Articles of incorporation: a document filed with a state agency to establish the existence of a corporation.

Articles of organization: a document filed with a state agency to establish the existence of a limited liability company. A LLC may elect to be managed by one or more managers by adding a statement to its articles of organization.

Assessor: an individual licensed by a state to value real property for the purpose of real property taxation. Some cottage LLCs use the property tax value set by an assessor to determine a cottage's value under buy-sell provisions of the operating agreement.

Beneficiary: a person who receives a benefit from a trust. In the cottage context, a person who has the right to use a cottage that is owned by a trust.

Branch: a multi-generational group of people in the same bloodline, each of whom shares a fractional interest in a cottage.

Branch ratio: the fraction of the cottage LLC owned by a branch.

Bylaws: one of the key documents of a corporation. The bylaws dictate the internal organization and operation of a corporation.

Cabbage: 1) a vacation home larger than a cabin but smaller than a cottage; 2) something that must be spent each year for the privilege of keeping a cottage.

Call option: the right, stated in a cottage LLC operating agreement, to force a member to sell his interest in the cottage LLC back to the company. The call option is triggered by a member's continuing default under the terms of the operating agreement. For example, a call option might take effect if a member failed to pay his share of the cottage expenses for two years.

Common law: a body of law developed over the course of centuries by court decisions. Common law is the source of the rights of owners of direct interests in real property. Although originally judge-made law, all states (other than Louisiana, a civil law state with common law elements) have incorporated common law into a network of statutes. Each state modifies the common law to carry out its policies. The "rules" described in Chapter 5 describe the common law rights and duties of tenants in common.

Cottage: for purposes of this book, a vacation home regardless of form, to be kept in the family for generations.

Cottage limited liability company (or cottage LLC): a limited liability company organized to own and operate a cottage.

Dynasty trust: a trust designed to hold assets for 100 or more years. Dynasty trusts seek to perpetuate family wealth free of transfer taxes, such as the estate and generation-skipping taxes. See "rule against perpetuities."

Estate promissory note: a debt that comes due only after the death of the person who created the obligation. For example, John signs a promissory note for $50,000 payable to the family's cottage limited liability company. At John's death, his estate owes $50,000 to the LLC.

Family limited partnership (FLP): a form of partnership authorized by statute that confers limited liability on at least one of the partners.

Fee tail: a common law form of ownership that confined the ownership of a parcel of real property to the descendants of a single individual. Fee tail evolved under the common law to keep property in a family. Fee tail, abolished by the states in the 18th and 19th centuries because it impaired the formation of capital, would have been great for cottage succession planning.

Founder: a person who establishes a cottage succession plan.

Heir: a person other than a founder who is a beneficiary of a cottage succession plan.

Immediate Cottage LLC: a cottage limited liability company that is formed during the lifetime of one or more of the founders. Compare "Springing Cottage LLC."

Irrevocable life insurance trust (ILIT): a trust that holds one or more life insurance policies. If properly established and funded, the death benefit is not subject to estate tax on the insured's death. ILITs are useful for creating an estate tax-free fund that may be used for family purposes, such as funding a cottage endowment, or paying the estate tax bill on a cottage.

Joint tenancy: one of the main forms of ownership of property under common law. The key feature of joint tenancy is that the owner who lives the longest automatically becomes the sole owner of the property. The "rules" described in Chapter 5 also apply to joint tenants. Compare tenancy in common and joint tenancy with right of survivorship.

Joint tenancy with right of survivorship (JTWROS): a special form of joint tenancy in effect in a small number of states, including Michigan. Although similar to joint tenancy in most respects, the remainder interests of property owned in JTWROS are not subject to partition.

Life estate: the right to use property for the life of a person. A life estate, which is one of the common law interests in property, may be measured by the life of any person. The life estate ends when that person dies. Life estates are sometimes used in cottage planning to guaranty the lifetime use of a cottage by a childless person.

Life tenant: the person who holds a life estate.

Limited liability company (LLC): a relatively new form of business organization that may be established under the laws of any state the United States. The members of a LLC are protected from the claims of a creditor of the organization.

Manager: a person or group of persons who controls the operation of a limited liability company. The scope of the manager's power is determined by the LLC's members.

Member: one of the owners of a limited liability company.

Millage: refers to the unit by which property tax is computed. One "mill" is $1/1,000^{th}$ of a dollar. If the millage rate is thirty-five, the property tax is computed by multiplying the property's taxable value by 0.035 (or 3.5%).

Operating agreement: the agreement, signed by the company's members, that governs a LLC. Typical operating agreements are twenty-five to thirty-five pages long.

Owelty: under common law, the amount that one owner must pay to another owner to settle accounts at the conclusion of a partition lawsuit.

Ownership agreement: an agreement between or among tenants in common or joint tenants who own a cottage.

Probate administration: the court-supervised process by which assets of a deceased person are distributed, and debts of a deceased person are paid. The court charged with oversight typically is called a "probate court."

Put option: an agreement that gives one person the right to force another to purchase something. In the cottage planning context, the right of a member of a cottage LLC to force the LLC or other members to buy the right-holder's membership interest in the LLC.

Qualified personal residence trust (QPRT): a limited duration trust designed to shift appreciation of a primary residence or cottage out of an owner's taxable estate. QPRTs, which are recognized in the Internal Revenue Code, were very popular in the 1990s, a time of rapid appreciation of real estate and relatively low estate tax exclusion amounts.

Remainderman/remaindermen: the person or persons who will acquire clear title to property when all life tenants of that property are dead.

Revocable living trust: a popular estate planning arrangement by which a person (the trustor, grantor, or settlor) transfers property (corpus, res) to a person (trustee) for the benefit of a person (the beneficiary). Assets titled in a revocable living trust are not subject to probate administration at the death of the trustor. Revocable living trusts are used by married couples to maximize the property that they may pass to their heirs free of estate tax.

Rule against perpetuities: a common law rule designed to prevent a person from tying up property in a trust indefinitely. The rule has been terminated by statute in some states (among them Alaska, Delaware, Idaho, Illinois, South Dakota and Wisconsin), thus permitting families to establish "dynasty trusts." Like fee tail, dynasty trusts one day will be prohibited under the policy against impairment of capital formation.

Shareholder: one of the owners of a corporation.

Spendthrift trust: an irrevocable trust established for the dual purposes of preventing a beneficiary from squandering the trust and preventing the beneficiary's creditors from attaching the beneficiary's interest in the trust.

Springing Cottage LLC: a succession plan under which the founder of a cottage succession plan transfers the cottage title to a revocable trust. The founder develops an operating agreement for a cottage LLC and attaches it to the trust as an exhibit. The trust directs the successor trustee to form a cottage LLC at the founder's death and distribute membership interests in the LLC to specified heirs. The heirs' relationship to the cottage is governed by the cottage LLC operating agreement developed by the founders.

Tenancy in common (TIC): a common law form of ownership the key feature of which is that each owner has the right to use the property at all times. The rules of TIC are described in Chapter 5.

Tenants in common: individuals who share ownership of property through tenancy in common.

Trustee: a person who holds property in trust for the benefit of another. See revocable living trust.

WHERE THE COTTAGES ARE

Florida leads in the number of seasonal recreational properties with 483,000 of them, followed by California (237,000), New York (235,000), and Michigan (234,000). Three New England states claim the highest saturation of cottages: sixteen percent of homes in Maine are cottages, followed by fifteen percent in Vermont, and ten percent in New Hampshire.

NOTES

This section provides support for statements made in the text. In preference to footnotes and endnotes, which seemed pedantic in a non-technical work, the end of the sentence to which reference is made is set in italics.

Introduction

5.2 million vacation homes in the United States: Di, McArdle and Masnick at 18.

600,000 in Canada: http://realtytimes.com/rtcpages/19990525_cottagers.htm. The Canadian Coalition of Provincial Cottagers' Associations estimates that there are three million cottage users of 600,000 Canadian recreational properties. If the five users per cottage ratio applies south of the border, there are about 25 million cottage users in the United States.

2002 market research study: Ipsos Reid, "Cottages Staying in the Family for Better or Worse." This market research study of Canadian cottage owners is part of the Royal LePage Recreational Property Report 2002, and was released May 15, 2002.

130,000 potential partition disputes arise in the United States each year: Baucells and Lippman, at 1197 n.30.

Author's Note

Every state and the District of Columbia has adopted limited liability company statutes: National Conference of Commissioners on Uniform State Laws, Revised Uniform LLC Act, Prefatory Note (2005). The Revised Uniform LLC Act may be viewed at: http://www.law.upenn.edu/bll/ulc/ullca/2005annmtgdraft.htm

Chapter 2. Avoid the Worst: A Partition Parable

snarling German shepherds: Baucells and Lippman, at 1220. Although the mathematically inclined will find the application of John Nash's game theory to partition fascinating, the joy in this law review article lies in Appendix B, which tells the "rest of the story" of a famous partition case, *Delfino v Vealensis*, 436 A.2d 27 (Conn. 1980). The case, featured in a widely-used law school textbook, involved Angelo Delfino's attempt to develop a subdivision against the wishes of Helen Vealensis.

The root of the problem (beyond two incredibly stubborn personalities) was Helen's dissatisfaction with plaster work performed by Angelo when he built Helen's house. Helen sued Angelo for the construction defect and won a $5,000 judgment. Angelo, described by his lawyer as a person who never backed away from a fight, decided to get even with Helen, a junkyard operator described by her lawyer as "single, obese, and financially destitute," and as a person "who never agreed to anything." His method was simple: he bought from Helen's brother, Frank (oh, the perfidy), Frank's 15/48ths tenancy-in-common interest in Helen's house, and thirteen days later filed a partition suit against Helen (who owned another 15/48ths interest) and Helen's sister (who owned the rest).

Helen's lawyer, who later ascended to the bench, remembers the case vividly, in part because Helen's two German shepherds attacked him when he went to his client's house to discuss the case. Helen's brother Frank, who described the dogs as "really mean suckers," would have to sit in his car and honk the horn so that Helen could escort him into the house. And this was *before* Frank sold out to Angelo.

Helen lost the case in the trial court so she appealed to the Connecticut Supreme Court. To everyone's surprise (including her lawyer), the Supreme Court reversed the trial court's decision and ordered the land partitioned in kind (as sought by Helen) and not partitioned by sale. The Supreme Court remanded the matter to the trial court, whose task it was to figure out how the land could be shared by a residential subdivision and Helen's junkyard. The court appointed Max Reicher, a retired judge, as a trial referee to work out the division of the land. Judge Reicher went to inspect the property and was attacked by the German shepherds. To his credit, he was able to craft a physical division of the property.

Angelo, of course, didn't want Helen to benefit from his development, and arranged to separate Helen's property from his using a two-foot wide by 126-foot long strip of land. This strip kept Helen from using the road, sewer, and water that he brought into the new subdivision. Helen was forced to use her artesian well, a septic field, and an easement to reach the public highway.

Angelo sold the land to a development company and realized a thirty-three percent annualized return on his investment. Although Helen emerged from the seven-year process with an isolated and devalued lot, she probably felt like she had won this epic battle of wills.

Chapter 4. How a Plan Helps Save the Family Cottage

the right of property: Craig-Taylor, at 746 n.61, citing Sir William Blackstone, *Commentaries on the Law of England Book II*, Chapter 1, at 207 (Sharswood ed., 1889).

Chapter 5. No Plan? Then 600-Year-Old Law Controls the Cottage

probably more than 800 years: Carrozzo, at 433, 438.

From A to B and C: Thompson § 32.06(b)(2) n.48.

they inherit it from their parents: Powell § 50.02[6].

a relationship that disinherits first co-owner to die: Powell § 51.03[3].

a "manifest injustice": Thompson § 32.05 n.15.

conveyancing document: Thompson § 31.03; Powell §§ 50.02, 51.02[1].

Author's comment on the "rules"

Thompson aptly said:

As a preliminary matter, it may be observed that the law governing the relations between cotenants is marked by a degree of vagueness; rules are applied under all the circumstances. To an extent, this is unavoidable: many of the disputed relationships between cotenants are sorted out in the context of partition proceedings, which are equitable. Furthermore, the courts are understandably reluctant to assume a supervisory role in ongoing relationships marked by discord. The power of alienation and the right of partition, possessed by every cotenant (except tenants by the entirety), provide openings for exit from contentious relationships, and rules are sometimes applied with an eye to encouraging their exercise. Thompson § 32.07.

Notwithstanding this admonition, my "rules" attempt to distill 800 years of common law into a series of concise statements regarding the rights and obligations of tenants in common. I sometimes use Michigan law to support my examples. Because the law in your state may not be the same as it is in Michigan, or for that matter, because Michigan law may have changed since this book was printed, these rules should not be acted upon without the benefit of legal counsel.

Rule 1: Each tenant in common has a right of partition.

Powell § 50.07; Thompson § 38.03

In rare cases, a court may deny partition in the rare case in which it would cause prejudice or harm to the other owners. Thompson § 38.03 n.22.

The right to partition cannot be defeated merely by showing that it would be inconvenient, injurious, or even ruinous to another owner. Powell § 50.07[3] n.18.

orders the cottage sold: Powell § 50.07[5].

it is literally priceless: Craig-Taylor, at 758 n.127.

Partition is economically efficient: Craig-Taylor, at 765.

wins the asset in a partition sale: Craig-Taylor, at 770 n.198.

Rule 2: Each tenant in common owns an "undivided interest" in the cottage.

Powell § 50.03; Thompson § 32.07; 20 Am Jur 2d §§ 2, 42.

Example 1: Powell § 50.03[1] n.2; Thompson § 32.07 n.141.

Example 2: Id.

simultaneous right to use the cottage whenever they want: Id.

has use rights equal to the child with a ninety-nine percent interest: Id.

cottage expense in proportion to his ownership: 20 Am Jur 2d § 63.

Example 3: 20 Am Jur 2d §§ 41, 50.

Example 6: Powell § 50.05[2] n.5; Thompson § 32.07(e); 20 Am Jur 2d §102 n.7.

Rule 3: A tenant in common has the right to transfer his interest to any person at any time.

Powell § 50.02[9]. "Each tenant in common has title that is separate and distinct. In the absence of an agreement to sell the property together, each tenant in common is free to transfer or encumber the interest without the knowledge or consent of the other tenant or tenants in common." Thompson § 32.08(b) n.200.

Example 1: Powell § 50.02[9]; 20 Am Jur 2d § 93 n.2.

Example 2: Powell § 50.05[1].

Rule 4: A tenant in common does not owe rent to the other owners for using the cottage.

Powell § 50.03[1][a]; 20 Am Jur 2d § 48.

Example 1: *Id.*

Example 2: Powell § 50.03[1][b] n.9; 20 Am Jur 2d §§ 49, 50. But see *Wengel v Wengel*, 270 Mich App 86; 714 NW2d 371 (2006) ("all doubts arising out of the nature and character of possession should weigh against ouster"). Was Bob just joking around or was he really threatening his siblings? An ouster requires "some clear, positive, and unequivocal act which amounts to an open denial of the cotenant's rights." *Fenton v Miller*, 94 Mich 204; 53 NW 957 (1892). *Fenton* shows the extent to which a court will go to avoid finding an ouster in a family situation. The cases in which courts have refused to find an ouster as between separated (and presumably antagonistic) spouses who hold title as tenants in common further confirms the law's reluctance to find an ouster. 20 Am Jur 2d § 50 n.9.

Example 3: Powell § 50.03[1][a] n.5; 20 Am Jur 2d § 50 n.10.

Rule 5: A tenant in common may rent the cottage to third parties without the consent of the other owners.

Example 1: 20 Am Jur 2d §101. Thompson § 32.07(d) n.180, states "The power of one tenant in common to alienate that tenant's share includes the power to lease the share." Thus, Bob may lease his own interest (use rights) in the cottage to Ed. In the twenty-one states that follow the 1705 English Statute of Queen Anne, however, Bob must share the rent with his siblings. Thompson § 31.07(c) nn.274, 275; Powell §§ 50.04[1], *but see* 20 Am Jur 2d § 47 n.4.

Example 2: 20 Am Jur 2d § 100.

Rule 6: A tenant in common is not required to compensate another tenant for services associated with management of the cottage.

Andy and Bob are not obligated to compensate Carol for her extra work: Powell § 50.04[2] n. 14; 20 Am Jur 2d § 46.

Rule 7: A tenant in common is not entitled to reimbursement for improvements to the cottage. A tenant in common is not entitled to reimbursement for repairs unless the repairs are necessary to preserve the cottage.

Powell § 50.04[2] nn.10 & 11. "A man cannot be improved out of his estate; in other words, a cotenant cannot be compelled to contribute to the expenses of improvement, lest the costs reduce, or even destroy, the unrealized value of the undivided share. An improver dissatisfied with this rule can always exercise the right of partition." Thompson § 32.07(b) n.148.

Example 2:

the painting was necessary to preserve the cottage: Thompson § 31.07(b). "On the contrary, when the expenses are not discretionary, contribution should be enforced. Repairs needed to keep a structure wind and water tight are a case in point." Thompson § 32.07(b) n.148.

charging the brothers would be unfair: 50 Am Jur 2d § 51 nn.5 & 6.

Example 3:

repairs were necessary to preserve the cottage: Thompson § 32.07(b).

reasonable rental value of his use of the cottage: Powell § 50.04[4] n.13.

Rule 8: A tenant in common who pays a disproportionate share of expenses is not necessarily entitled to reimbursement.

Example 1:

Bob is entitled to reimbursement for property taxes: Powell § 50.04[2] n.16; Thompson § 32.07(b) n.149; 20 Am Jur 2d § 67.

mortgage or insurance payments: 20 Am Jur 2d § 65; but see Thompson § 31.07(b) n.269.

extra use of the cottage was sufficient compensation. The commentators disagree on this point: Thompson § 31.07(a) n.260.

Example 2: Thompson § 32.07(b) n.151.

Rule 9: A tenant in common has only limited duties to the other tenants in common.

Commentators cannot agree if tenants in common are fiduciaries. Thompson leans against their being fiduciaries, with Powell suggesting that they probably are. Thompson §§ 31.07(b), 32.07(b) nn.154-156; Powell § 50.04[3]. American Jurisprudence 2nd finds a "relationship of mutual trust and confidence as to the common estate" but stops short of declaring tenants in common to be fiduciaries. 20 Am Jur 2d § 3 n.2. Michigan's John Cameron, another well-regarded commentator, labels the relationship of tenants in common "special." Cameron § 9.5.

no duty to insure their interest in the property: 20 Am Jur 2d § 41 n.16.

Chapter 6. Other Animals in the Property Law Zoo

Joint tenancy

The nine rules described in Chapter 5 also apply to joint tenants: Powell § 51.03[4].

Example 1: Powell § 51.03[3].

Example 2: Powell § 51.03[3] n.10.

Example 3: Powell § 51.04[1] n.16; Thompson § 31.08(b) nn.321-323; Michigan Land Title Standards, Standard 6.3, Problem B.

Example 4: Powell § 51.04[2] n.42.

Example 5: Powell § 51.03[3].

Joint tenancy with right of survivorship

From A to B and C and to the survivor of them: Michigan Land Title Standards, Standard 6.4.

JTWROS prevents a full partition of their interests: Michigan recognizes two forms of joint tenancy. A conveyance to A and B "as joint tenants and not as tenants in common" creates the traditional joint tenancy, which can be severed and partitioned by any of the cotenants at any time. But a conveyance to A and B "and the survivor of them" or to A and B "as joint tenants with right of survivorship" gives A and B a joint life estate along with contingent remainders awarding the fee simple to whichever cotenant lives longer. A and B can sever and partition the life estate and they can alienate the contingent remainders, but the owner of the fee will ultimately depend on which of the original grantees survives the other. If A conveys all his interest to C and B conveys all her interest to D, and A then dies before B, D will own the fee and C will have nothing. Cooper, Continuing Problems with Michigan's Joint Tenancy "With Right of Survivorship," 78 Mich BJ 966 (1999).

Example 3: Cooper, at 966, citing *Albro v Allen*, 434 Mich 271; 454 NW2d 85 (1990).

Example 4: *Albro v Allen,* supra.

Example 5: Cameron, § 9.11.

Tenancy by the entireties

a special form of ownership that exists in thirty states: Carrozzo at 445 nn.219-221. Thirteen states have abolished tenancy by the entireties. Carrozzo at 446 n.224. The status of tenancy by the entireties is uncertain in the remaining seven states. Carrozzo at 446 n.225.

called for its abolition: Carrozzo at 456 nn.315-321.

Community Property

used only in Arizona, California, Idaho, Louisiana, Nevada, New Mexico, Texas, Washington, and Wisconsin: Powell § 53.01[1] n.6.

("community property") is deemed to be owned equally by each spouse: Powell § 53.01[2].

each of the couple's assets is placed into one of three categories: his *separate property*, her *separate property*, and their *community property*: Powell § 53.01[4].

surviving spouse may control the deceased spouse's interest in community property: Powell § 53.09[2].

a resident of Louisiana, Texas, or Wisconsin who dies without a last will and testament passes to his statutory heirs: Powell § 53.09[4] n.38.

Example 1: Powell § 53.03[1][a] n.2.

Example 2: Powell § 53.03[1][c] n.55.1 & 56.

Chapter 7. Short-Term Solutions

Using life estates

C pays the property taxes: A life tenant must pay real estate tax unless the deed provides otherwise. 51 Am Jur 2d § 121; 28 Am Jur 2d 113 (in some states, failure to pay property taxes constitutes waste, justifying forfeiture of the estate to remaindermen); *but see* 28 Am Jur 2d § 112; Cameron § 7.8, citing *Rolland v Rolland*, 314 Mich 619, 23 NW2d 104 (1946).

[C pays the] maintenance: 51 Am Jur 2d § 28 n.10.

may make improvements to the cottage: 51 Am Jur 2d § 33.

C is not obligated to insure the cottage but may do so: Cameron § 7.8, citing *In re Cameron's Estate*, 158 Mich 174, 122 NW 564 (1909). If insurance proceeds in excess of the life tenant's interest are received by the life tenant, he must remit the balance to the remainderman. *Blanchard v Kingston*, 222 Mich 631, 193 NW 241 (1923).

Example 1: *Bob knows his right to use the cottage cannot be taken away even if Andy and Carol sell the cottage*: 28 Am Jur 2d § 62.

Example 2: 28 Am Jur 2d § 61 n.72.

The Ownership Agreement

Thompson § 32.06(a) n.28.

provided circumstances haven't changed since the agreement was signed: Thompson § 31.08(b) n.343.

Chapter 8. Choose the Right Business Entity for Your Cottage

The Limited Liability Company

LLC is the fastest-growing business form in the country: CCH Business Owner's Toolkit: Comparing the LLC and the Corporation. www.toolkit.cch.com

is proof it delivers these promised benefits: Kleinrock, Federal Tax Expert §§ 202.2(a) and 451.1.

The state filing fee usually is less: CCH Business Owner's Toolkit: Initial State Filing Fees for Forming a Business Entity, *id*. One notable exception is Massachusetts. The fee to form a corporation is $275 and the fee to form an LLC is $500. The annual filing fees in Massachusetts are $125 for a corporation and $500 for an LLC. New York requires an LLC to publish information from its articles of organization once per week for six weeks in two newspapers. The cost of publication ranges from $1,000 to $2,000. Arizona and Nebraska impose a comparable requirement on corporations and limited liability companies. Pennsylvania imposes the publication requirement only on corporations. A statutory close corporation may be less expensive in these states. CCH Business Owner's Toolkit: State Fees for LLCs and Corporations, *id*.

Comparing the LLC to the Pretenders

rented for less than fifteen days each year: IRC Section 280A refers to properties owned by "individuals or a S corporation (IRC § 280A(a)). The Internal Revenue Service used its rule-making power to extend the benefits and burdens of Section 280A to pass-through entities, such as partnerships, trusts, and estates, through regulations. Prop. Reg. § 1.280A-1(e)(5)(i). Although the proposed regulation does not mention limited liability companies (it was adopted in 1975 — the first LLC came into existence in 1977), Section 280A does applies to cottages owned by LLCs because LLCs are pass-through entities. It is not entirely clear how the personal use rules apply to vacation homes owned by entities such as partnerships and LLCs. BNA 547-2nd at n.96.

Chapter 9. Welcome to the Club

Like a private club, the members of a limited liability company decide who may become a member: The LLC operating agreement may contain any provision that is not prohibited by law. Revised Uniform Limited Liability Company Act (2005) §110. Limiting the identity of permissible members is not prohibited, therefore the operating agreement may impose this restriction.

Chapter 10. When and How to Organize the Cottage LLC

1. Choosing a state

such as sale of the cottage or dissolution of the company: Revised Uniform Limited Liability Company Act (2005) §§ 407(b)(3)(B) and 407(b)(3)(D).

Some states (most famously, Delaware): See, for instance, Section 18-402 of the Delaware Limited Liability Company Act, which allows the managers to make all decisions for the company (thus barring the members from voting).

5. Transfer the cottage property to the LLC

purchase an endorsement from the insurance company that names the cottage LLC as an additional insured. One case held that a transfer of land from two family members to a LLC, of which they were the only members, terminated coverage under a policy naming the individual family members as the insured parties. *Gebhardt Family Restaurant, L.L.C. v Nation's Title Ins. Co. of New York*, 132 Md App 457, 752 A.2d 1222, 1226-27 (2000), cited in Murray, Title Insurance Endorsements for Limited Liability Transactions. First American Title Co. (2001). http://www.firstam.com/content.cfm?id=2912

"non-imputation endorsement": id.

7. Issue membership certificates to owners

it is less likely that fractional units will be required: Raising prime numbers to an exponent guarantees that fractional units will not be required for a long time (seven generations if each set of parents produces one or two children, five generations in which a set of parents has three children, and so on). Here is a method I use to determine the number of membership units to be created:

$$2^7 \times 3^5 \times 5^3 \times 7^2 = 100,352,000 \text{ units}$$

Chapter 11. The Cottage Safety Valve

over eighty percent of cottages are owned free and clear: Di, McArdle and Masnick at 16.

Chapter 12. Cottage Democracy

A tip of the hat to the Hanawalt clan for suggesting the "MOM" (Maintenance and Operations Manager).

Chapter 14. Renting the Cottage

Insurance

It is stupid to game the system: Magnotta v Michigan Millers Insurance Co, 35 Mich App 450; 192 NW2d 553 (1971).

Structuring to limit liability of owners to renters

series LLC: Delaware Limited Liability Company Act § 18-215. This controversial law was criticized by the American Bar Association Committee on Partnerships and Unincorporated Business Organizations in its March, 2006 report. Delaware's "series" LLC provisions were excluded intentionally from the 2006 Revised Uniform LLC Act by the Uniform Law Commission, which commented: "What's good for Delaware and highly sophisticated deals is not necessarily good for the LLC law of other states. A philosophy that works wonders for 'high end' transactions may be bad medicine for the thousands of more prosaic but nonetheless important closely held businesses that choose to house themselves within LLCs."

Chapter 15. Minimizing the Federal Tax Bite

Using annual exclusion gifts to transfer the cottage tax free

Test 1: The Hackls and the present interest requirement: *Hackl v Commissioner,* 118 T.C. 279 (2002); 335 F3d 664 (7th Cir. 2003).

a burden the Hackls have not met: Hackl v Commissioner, 335 F3d 664, 667 (7th Cir. 2003).

Test 2: The Tehans and the retained interest problem: *Tehan v Commissioner,* T.C. Memo 2005-128 (5/31/2005).

deploy its enforcement resources against a family that has not observed the requisite formalities: The IRS won a similar case in 2006 because the taxpayer did not pay fair market rent to the general partnership (unfortunately named "Funny Hats") that owned her home. *Disbrow v CIR,* T.C. Memo 2006-24.

The Internal Revenue Service has shown some flexibility in vacation home cases, ruling that, where a woman gave her vacation home to her children but retained the right to use the home in December, only 1/12th of the value of the home would be included in the woman's taxable estate. Rev. Rul 79-108, 1979-1 C.B. 75. Discussed at BNA 50-5th at n. 218.

On the other hand, where the amount of time that the parent could use a vacation property was not limited, and the parent did not pay fair market rent, the Internal Revenue Service has argued successfully that the entire property should be included in the deceased parent's estate notwithstanding the purported gift of the property to a descendant. Courts repeatedly have found an implied agreement between the donor-parent and donee-child to allow the parent to use the property for the rest of the parent's lifetime. The right to use the property justifies its inclusion in the deceased parent's taxable estate despite the paper gift. BNA 50-5th at nn.874-875 and BNA 800-2nd at nn.953-955.

or pay a fair market rent to the company for their use of the cottage: BNA 50-5th at n.877.

The Price Tag on Cottage Units

unless you fully understand the audit and litigation risks involved: In FSA 200049003, which was released before the IRS victory in *Strangi v Commissioner,* 417 F.3d 468 (5th Cir. 2005), the IRS expessed hostility to valuation discounts taken by a family LLC. See also *Dailey v Commissioner,* T.C. Memo 2002-301, a family limited partnership case.

The Internal Revenue Service published regulations in 1994 to prevent taxpayers from achieving "tax results that were not intended by Congress" through the formation of business entities such as partnerships and limited liability companies. Treas. Reg. Section 1.701-2. The preamble to the final regulation stated that the anti-abuse rules would extend to the operation of the gift tax. The Service initially took the position that the anti-abuse rules would come into play because the partnership did not have a business purpose, but later retreated from this position. It is not, therefore, the Service's current position that you must prove that your cottage LLC has a business purpose in order for gifts of interests in the LLC to be valid, or for you to take appropriate valuation discounts with respect to those gifts. BNA 812-2nd at n.348.

Appraisals and IRS Reporting

IRS does not accept values set by tax assessors for estate or gift tax purposes: Frazee v Commissioner, 98 T.C. 554 (1992).

and information on valuation discounts: Treas. Reg. § 301.6501(c)-1. To satisfy this requirement, the gift tax return must contain the following information: (1) a description of the transferred property and any consideration received by the transferor; (2) the identity of, and relationship between, the transferor and the transferee; (3) if property is transferred in trust, the trust's tax identification number and a brief description of the trust terms (or a copy of the trust instrument); (4) a detailed description of the method used to determine the fair market value of the property transferred; and (5) a statement describing any position that is contrary to any proposed, temporary, or final regulations or revenue rulings published at the time of the transfer.

Chapter 16. The Ultimate Gift: A Cottage Endowment

Projected rate of return and inflation rate

the average appreciation rate for the Standard and Poors 500 stock index has been twelve percent: Ibbotson.

The author has written a spreadsheet that may be used to compute the size of an endowment that a family must create to make its cottage self-supporting. Available for download at www.cottagelaw.com on the "Resources" tab.

Irrevocable life insurance trust

excellent tool to create and manage a cottage endowment: A recent case, *Chawala v Transamerica Occidental Life Insurance Co*, 440 F3d 639 (4th Cir 2006) casts doubt on whether an ILIT has an insurable interest in the life of the insured. Estate planning attorneys are seeking legislation to remove the uncertainly caused by this surprising case.

BIBLIOGRAPHY

Treatises

American Jurisprudence, 2nd *Cotenancy and Joint Ownership*, Rochester, NY: Lawyers Co-operative Publishing Company, 2007 (cited as 20 Am Jur 2d).

American Jurisprudence, 2nd *Estates*, Rochester, NY: Lawyers Co-operative Publishing Company, 2007 (cited as 28 Am Jur 2d).

American Jurisprudence, 2nd *Life Tenants and Remaindermen*, Rochester, NY: Lawyers Co-operative Publishing Company, 2007 (cited as 51 Am Jur 2d).

Cameron, John G., Jr. *Michigan Real Estate Law*, 3rd ed. Ann Arbor: Institute for Continuing Legal Education, 2005.

O'Neal, F.H. and Robert B. Thompson. *O'Neal's Oppression of Minority Shareholders*, 2nd ed. Deerfield, IL: Clark Boardman Callaghan, 1992.

Powell, Richard R. *The Law of Real Property*, Rohan ed. New York: Matthew Bender, 2007.

Restatement of the Law of Property. St. Paul, MN: American Law Institute, 1936.

Thompson, George. 4 *Thompson on Real Property*, 2nd Thomas ed. Philadelphia: Lexis Law Publishing, 2007.

Books

Arnold, Elizabeth. *Creating the Good Will*. New York: Penguin Group (USA)-Portfolio, 2005.

Baines, Barry K. *Ethical Wills: Putting Your Values on Paper*, 2nd ed. Cambridge, MA: DaCapo Press, 2006.

Balfe, Judith Huggins. *Passing It On: The Inheritance and Use of Summer Houses*. Montclair, NJ: Pocomo Press, 1999.

Barney, Colleen and Victoria Collins. *Best Intentions: Ensuring Your Estate Plan Delivers Both Wealth and Wisdom*. Chicago: Dearborn Trade Publishing, 2002.

Biancalana, Joseph. *The Fee Tail and the Common Recovery in Medieval England, 1176-1502*. Cambridge, UK: Cambridge University Press, 2001.

Cambridge, James R. and George J. Christopoulos. *Michigan Limited Liability Companies*, 2nd ed. Ann Arbor: Institute for Continuing Legal Education, 2005.

Casner, A. James and W. Barton Leach. *Cases and Text on Real Property*, 2nd ed. Boston: Little, Brown & Co, 1969.

Cecil, Evelyn. *Primogenture: A Short History of Its Development in Various Countries, and Its Practical Effects*. London: J. Murray, 1895.

Choate, Natalie B. *The QPRT Manual*. Boston: Ataxplan Publications, 2004.

Clarke, Alison and Paul Kohler. *Property Law*. Cambridge, UK: Cambridge University Press, 2005.

Collier, Charles W. *Wealth in Families*, 2nd ed. Cambridge: Harvard University, 2006.

Condon, Gerald M. and Jeffrey L. Condon. *Beyond the Grave: The Right Way and the Wrong Way of Leaving Money to Your Children (and Others)*. New York: HarperCollins, 2001.

Fellows, Deborah Wyatt. *reflections of a life up north*. Traverse City, MI: Prism Publications, 2004.

Fish, Barry and Les Kotzer. *The Family Fight: Planning to Avoid It*, 2nd ed. Washington, DC: Continental Atlantic Productions, 2003.

Fithian, Scott C. *Values-Based Estate Planning*. New York: John Wiley and Sons, 2000.

Huggins, Ken, and Judith Huggins Balfe. *How to Pass It On: The Ownership and Use of Summer Houses*. (64-page workbook) New Jersey: Pocomo Press, 1999.

Hunter, Douglas. *The Cottage Ownership Guide: How to Buy, Sell, Rent, Share, Hand Down & Retire to Your Waterfront Getaway*, Buffalo, NY: Cottage Life Books, 2006.

Ibbotson Associates, *Stocks, Bonds, Bills and Inflation 2007 Yearbook*, Chicago: Ibbotson Associates, 2007.

Jurinski, James John and Gary A. Zwick. *Transferring Interests in the Closely Held Family Business*. Philadelphia: ALI-ABA, 2002.

Karpinski, Christine Hrib. *How to Rent Vacation Properties by Owner*. Woodstock, GA: Kinney Pollack Press, 2004.

Koski, Nikki. *The Cottage Rules: An Owner's Guide to the Rights and Responsibilities of Sharing Recreational Property*. Bellingham, WA: Self-Counsel Press, 2005.

Marans, R.W. and J.D. Wellman. *The Quality of Non-Metropolitan Living*. Ann Arbor, MI: University of Michigan Survey Research Center, 1978.

Palmisano, Joanne. *Camps, Cottages and Cabins: Your Seasonal Home Handbook*. Burlington, VT: Happy Hollow Productions, 2002.

Rosenthal, Lois. *Partnering: A Guide to Co-Owning Anything from Homes to Home Computers.* Cincinnati: Writer's Digest Books, 1983.

Shammas, Carole, Marylynn Salmon, and Michel Dahlin. *Inheritance in America from Colonial Times to the Present.* New Brunswick, NJ: Rutgers University Press, 1987.

Small, Steven J. *Preserving Family Lands: Book I; Essential Tax Strategies for the Landowner,* 2nd ed. Boston: Landowner Planning Center, 1992.

Small, Steven J. *Preserving Family Lands: Book II; More Planning Strategies for the Future.* Boston: Landowner Planning Center, 1997.

Small, Steven J. *Preserving Family Lands: Book III; New Tax Rules and Strategies and a Checklist.* Boston: Landowner Planning Center, 2002.

Stynes, Daniel J., JiaJia Zheng, and Susan I. Stewart. *Seasonal Homes in Michigan.* East Lansing, MI: Michigan State University, 1995.

Wood, Robert W. *Home Office, Vacation Home, and Home Rental Deductions.* BNA Tax Management Portfolios: 547-2nd. Rockville, MD: BNA, 2004.

Articles

Baucells, Manel and Stephen A. Lippman. "Justice Delayed Is Justice Denied: A Cooperative Game Theoretic Analysis of Hold-Up in Co-Ownership." 22 *Cardozo L. Rev.* 1191 (2000-2001). This is the article that applies the Nash equilibrium to bargaining in a partition case.

Baumann, Timothy R. "Note: Family Limited Partnerships, Trusts, or Limited Liability Corporations: Which Should the Elderly Choose." 3 *Elder L J* 111 (1995).

Bearup, George F. "Recent Developments in Family Limited Partnership Drafting." 13th Annual Drafting Estate Planning Documents Seminar. Institute for Continuing Legal Education. (Ann Arbor, January 15, 2004).

Carr, Tom. "Passing on the Keys." *Traverse City Record-Eagle*, July 23, 2006.

Carroll, John. "My (Other) House." *American Demographics*, June 2002, 43.

Carrozzo, Peter M. "Tenancies in Antiquity: A Transformation of Concurrent Ownership for Modern Relationships." 85 *Marquette L Rev* 423, (2001).

Cole, Steven R. "Due Diligence and Joint Ownership Agreements." *Buying and Selling Vacation Property: What Every Lawyer Should Know*. Institute for Continuing Legal Education. (Ann Arbor, February 22, 2002).

Cooper, Byron D. "Continuing Problems with Michigan's Joint Tenancy with Right of Survivorship." 78 *Mich B J* 966 (September, 1999).

Craig-Taylor, Phyliss. "Through a Colored Looking Glass: A View of Judicial Partition, Family Land Loss, and Rule Setting." 78 *Wash U L Q* 737 (2000).

Curry, Pat. "Second to None." *Builder*, October 2003, 218.

Darlin, Damon. "With a little estate planning, your house can stay in the family." *New York Times*, January 21, 2006.

Dew, Thomas E. "Tax Notes: Sharing the Family's Wealth: A Family LLC Is Still an Attractive Way to Make Annual Exclusion Gifts." 81 *Mich B J* 50 (2002).

Di, Zhu Xiao, Nancy McArdle and George S. Masnick. "Second Homes: What, How Many, Where and Who." Joint Center for Housing Studies of Harvard University (February, 2001).

Forrest, Diane. "Heartaches and Headaches: The sticky business of handing down the cottage." *Cottage Life*, May 1997, 36.

Francese, Peter. "The Second Home Boom." *American Demographics*, June 2003, 40.

Goffe, Wendy S. "Vacation Property: Planning Strategies for Keeping the Vacation Home in the Family." 32 *Estate Planning* 3 (September 2005).

Goffe, Wendy S. "Keeping the Cabin in the Family: A Guide to Joint Ownership and Use." 31 *ACTEC Journal* 89 (2005).

Ilardi, Jr., Anthony. "Use and Impact of Michigan Limited Liability Companies in Estate Planning." 1993 Advanced Estate Planning Institute, Institute for Continuing Legal Education. (Ann Arbor, 1993).

Internal Revenue Service, "Publication 527: Residential Real Property (Including Rental of Vacation Homes).

Irish, Michael W. "Planning and Drafting for the Michigan Vacation Home." 12 *Mich Prob & Tr LJ* 5 (Winter 1993).

Johnson, Kenneth M. and Calvin L. Beale. "Nonmetro Recreation Counties: Their Identification and Rapid Growth." *Rural America* 17, No. 4 (Winter, 2002).

Karjala, Dennis S. "An Analysis of Close Corporation Legislation in the United States." 21 *Ariz St LJ* 663 (Fall 1989).

Kennedy, Ian. "Trusting Your Cottage in a Cottage Trust (unpublished ms).

Kramer, Louise. "Paradise Lost." *Worth Magazine*, December 2005, 102.

Lawyer, Jeffrey T. "Vacation Homes and *Bolton v. Comm'r*: The Right Result for the Wrong Reasons." 1985 *Duke L J* 793 (1985).

Lund, Thomas. "The Modern Mind of the Medieval Attorney." 64 *Tex L Rev* 1267 (1986). A lawyer finds humor in ancient English real property cases.

MacDonald, Gayle. "Share Wars." *Cottage Life*. April/May 1993, 54.

Martin, John H. "Preserving the Family Vacation Home for Future Generations, 21 *Mich Prob & Tr LJ* 8 (Spring 2002).

McGranahan, David A. "Natural Amenities Drive Rural Population Change." USDA Agricultural Economic Report 781. September, 1999.

Mehallow, Cindy. "Vacation Homes Present Second Set of Issues for Seniors." *Chicago Tribune*, July 23, 2003.

Pierson, David. "Short-Term Rental Restrictions in Single Family Zones – A Growing Battle for Control of the Lakeshore. 30 *Mich Real Prop Rev* 61 (2003).

Redmond, Luanne Bethke. "Land, Law, and Love." 11 *Persuasions* 46-52, 1989. (A publication of the Jane Austen Society).

Reeder, Richard J. and Dennis M. Brown. "Recreation, Tourism, and Rural Well-Being." USDA Economic Research Report 7, August, 2005.

Scott, John A. "Simple Client Wishes with Complicated Drafting Implications." 12th Annual Drafting Estate Planning Documents Seminar Handbook, at 86. Institute for Continuing Legal Education (Ann Arbor, 2003).

Scott, John A. "Transferring Vacation Property to a Family Trust or LLC." Proceedings of the 45th Annual Probate and Estate Planning Institute, Probate and Estate Planning Section of the State Bar of Michigan and the Michigan Judicial Institute, at 685 (Ann Arbor, 2005).

Stake, Jeffrey Evans. "Evolution of Rules in a Common Law System: Differential Litigation of the Fee Tail and other Perpetuities, in Symposium: The Behavioral Analysis of Legal Institution: Possibility, Limitation, and New Direction Judicial Decisionmaking" 32 *Fl State U Law Rev* 401 (2005).

Van Eenenaam, John. "Drafting the Personal Residence or 'Cottage' Trust." Drafting Estate Planning Documents III, Institute of Continuing Education (Ann Arbor, 1994).

Walmsley, Ann. "How to Succeed at Succession." *Cottage Life*, April/May 2002, 54.

Whitaker, G. Warren. "Classic Issues in Family Succession Planning." 17 *Prob & Prop* 32 (2003). A lawyer finds timeless lessons in stories from the Book of Genesis and Shakespeare.

Windsor, Shawn. "All in the Family: When Inheriting Vacation Property, Be Prepared to Set Rules, Get Along." *Detroit Free Press*, July 22, 2005 (online edition).

Internet

Douglas, Ann. "The Cottage Contract." *Canadian Parents Online,* September 12, 2004.

http://lifewise.canoe.ca/LifewiseFamilymatters0205/02_cottage2-par.html

Reddy, Thrupthi. "Keeping Vacation Homes Peaceful." *Wealth Management Letter,* April 13, 2005 enews.prismb2b.com/enews/registeredrep/wealth_manager/2005_04_13_4132005/display

Sichelman, Lew. "The Second Home Market Older, Larger Than Thought." *Realty Times,* November 27, 2002. http://realtytimes.com/rtnews/rtcpages/20021127_secondhome.htm

Acknowledgments

I started visiting the Lake Superior shore in 1989. It is a beautiful and wild place with, as they like to say, "Nature in Abundance." I had my I-must-do-cottage law epiphany during my 2001 retreat and started this book while there the next fall. The residents of Grand Marais were most hospitable, and perhaps a little amused, by the troll lawyer[1] who spent beautiful autumn days hunched over a laptop computer. Mikel Classen, a writer from Grand Marais, gave me some much needed encouragement at a time when writing an entire book seemed too big an undertaking for me to complete in a lifetime of fall weeks. The Bird Boys kept me going too, but in a different way. Thanks, lads.

Many of the concepts presented in this book evolved through discussions with cottage families. While I wish I could thank them by name, attorney-client privilege comes first. You know who you are. I am honored to have been entrusted with your cottage's future.

I express my gratitude to Deb Fellows, whose graceful foreword reminds us why it is worth making the effort to save the family cottage. Her prose and Up North sensibility inspires us.

A number of people graciously took time from their schedules to answer my questions. Brian Price of the Leelanau Conser-

---

1 Residents of Michigan's Upper Peninsula call people from the Lower Peninsula "trolls" because they live below the Mackinac Bridge.

vancy described how conservation easements apply to lakefront property, and Professor Ted Ligibel explained how historic preservation and façade easements could help preserve family cottages by reducing their values for tax purposes. Rod Kurtz, Peter Haller, Jim McGovern, Rob DeLonge, and Susan Sheldon, helped me understand the trust officer's view of the family cottage.

Lawyers are afraid of new and untested things. I bear full responsibility for any errors of law contained in this book, but derive comfort from the fact that the manuscript was reviewed by Peter Doren and John MacNeal, partners in the Traverse City firm Sondee, Racine & Doren, PLC, to which I am of counsel. Special thanks to Peter for explaining to me the difference between a pig and a hog. Attorney Fred Bimber coached me on the bankruptcy and creditor protection aspects of the limited liability company, for which I thank him. My thanks as well to Steve Chambers for his perceptive comments on the manuscript.

John Martin helped me see the family cottage from a Realtor's perspective and was kind enough to dig through the archives in search of the perfect cottage photograph.

On the editorial side, this book's nonlinear path through the word garden was guided by Lori Hall Steele, whose editing helped transform my dry prose into something readable, by Shelley Watkins and Doug Truax, whose editorial counsel on my earliest drafts nudged me in the right direction, and by Amanda Holmes and Dan Stewart, who helped assemble pieces into a workable whole. My daughter, Catherine, who at nineteen is a formidable writer, offered great suggestions on the manuscript, as did my old friends, Rachel Markun and Carol Bawden.

Angela Saxon, of Saxon Design, designed the book cover, the book interior, and drew the illustrations. If Angela ever gets tired of these roles, she can launch a new career as a mind-reader. She grasped my vision for the book instantly and brought it to fruition effortlessly, on time, and on budget. I am also indebted to Aimé Merizon for her punctilious proofreading, and to Rick and Susan Cover, Colleen Christensen, and Sharon Sutterfield for making the photo shoot memorable.

Paul Sutherland, CFP, and Phil Hamburg were kind to take the time to explain to Rose and me the Byzantine world of book development, distribution, and promotion. It helps to have had a lamp in the darkness.

Karen Schaub, my office administrator, proved her value again by keeping the office running smoothly when I was "off task." Thank you, Karen, for your general excellence and for shifting the weight of administering a law office from my shoulders to yours.

Jon Roth made many contributions to cottage law and to the development of this book. An heir who understands all facets of the cottage dynamic, Jon developed the website cottagelaw.com (and its affiliate cottagemediation.com), encouraged me to write this book, and made insightful comments on the manuscript.

My friend, Bruce Douglass, shares my interest in cottage family dynamics. By virtue of his training as a psychologist, Bruce, a cottage founder himself, understands why parents, children, siblings, and cousins don't always get along. Bruce's companionship at our cottage seminars has made the enterprise more enjoyable. A fine Scotch, a Honduran cigar, intelligent company, a starlit evening at the cottage – here's to more of that, friend.

Finally — and most importantly — to my wife, Rose, whose company has made the last twenty-eight years more fun and tastier (she is a chef) than I could have ever hoped for, my heartfelt appreciation for placing your aspirations on hold to bring this book into the world. Everyone tells me that I am lucky you are my partner and the mother of our children. They are so right. It will be fun to see where this book takes us.

Appendix

Table of Contents
Cottage Limited Liability Company
Operating Agreement

4. Rights, Allocations, and Distributions
4.1. Rights
    4.1.1. Members
    4.1.2. Guests of members
    4.1.3. Rental
4.2. Allocatins
4.3. Distributions
4.4. Damage

5. Withdrawal; Transfer of Membership Interests
5.1. Restriction on Transfer
5.2. Permitted Transfers
5.3. Transfers Permitted on Condition
5.4. Rules Applicable to This Article
5.5. Put Option
5.6. Purchase Price and Terms
    5.6.1. Price
    5.6.2. Terms
5.7. Supplemental Assessment Arising from Certain Transfers
5.8. Company-Owned Life Insurance

6. Decisions of Members
6.1. Voting; Voting Table
6.2. Meetings
6.3. Consent
6.4. Voting by Legally Disabled Persons; Agents
6.5. Matters to be Decided Only by Members

7. Management
7.1. Management
    7.1.1. Qualifying as a manager
    7.1.2. Selection and replacement of managers
    7.1.3. Term of office
    7.1.4. Meetings
    7.1.5. Making decisions
    7.1.6. Designated responsibilities of individual managers
    7.1.7. Overlapping duties of managers
7.2. General Powers of Management Committee
7.3. Limitations
7.4. Standard of Care
7.5. No Authority of Members
7.6. Reimbursement
7.7. Registered Agent

Index

Note: **Boldfaced** page numbers indicate definitions.

About the Author

Stuart J. Hollander spent his summers in northern Michigan on Elk Lake and Torch Lake. A graduate of the University of Michigan and the University of California, Hastings College of the Law, the author was a partner in an international law firm in San Francisco before returning to live in northern Michigan in 1989. The focus of his practice is cottage law.

The author is a member of the Tax Court, the State Bars of Michigan and California, the Probate & Estate and Real Property Sections of the State Bar of Michigan, and the Estate Planning, Trust and Probate Law Section of the State Bar of California.

The author practices in an old railroad depot in Suttons Bay. The building, which is on the National Register of Historic Places and the Michigan Register of Historic Places, was built in 1920 by Leelanau County residents from native fieldstone.

The author has spoken on cottage law to a number of groups, including lake associations, historical societies, and professional organizations such as the Real Property Section of the State Bar of Michigan. He has been interviewed by many publications on the subject of cottage succession planning.

Evidence of the author's summers in northern Michigan — and more information about cottage law — may be found on the firm's website: **www.cottagelaw.com.**